FAST FOOD FACTS

FIFTH EDITION

The Original Guide for Fitting Fast
Food Into a Healthy Lifestyle

MARION J. FRANZ MS, RD, LD, CDE

IDC Publishing
MINNEAPOLIS

© 1998 International Diabetes Center
Institute for Research and Education HealthSystem Minnesota

IDC Publishing
3800 Park Nicollet Boulevard
Minneapolis, Minnesota 55416-2699
(612) 993-3393
www.idcpublishing.com

Printed in the United States of America

Publisher: Karol Carstensen
Production Manager: Gail Devery
Associate Editor: Sara Frueh
Cover and Text Design: MacLean & Tuminelly

ISBN 1-885115-43-1

Table of Contents

Acknowledgments

I would like to thank the following for their invaluable assistance in completing this book. A special thanks to the many restaurants that provided us with nutrition information about their menu items. Without their willingness to share their nutritional data this book would be impossible. Thanks also to dietetic students Stephanie Olson and LeAnn Reinhardt for their willing and capable assistance in the early stages of draft development.

I'd also like to acknowledge my colleagues—the skilled dietitians at the International Diabetes Center who are a constant source of encouragement and support as we endeavor to provide people with relevant, up-to-date information about nutrition in general and nutrition and diabetes in particular. A heart-felt thanks to the publishing department, Karol Carstensen, director of IDC Publishing, Gail Devery, and Sara Frueh, for their ideas, editorial suggestions, and careful considerations. Last but not least, I'd like to thank the rest of the International Diabetes Center staff for their continued interest and encouragement in these publishing ventures.

Finally, thank you, readers, for making *Fast Food Facts* such a success. I hope this new edition is especially helpful to you as you seek to eat wisely and live well.

Marion J. Franz, MS, RD, LD, CDE

Introduction

A recent survey reported that Americans eat out more than nine times weekly and that three out of four consumers dine regularly at fast-food restaurants. Because we eat out at such a high rate, the fat and calories in fast foods can cause problems when it comes to our waistlines and our health.

But how can we make better choices when the fat and calories are so difficult to decipher? Is the hamburger patty four ounces or six? Is the slice of cheese on the cheeseburger one ounce or two?

Help is not only on the way, it's right here in your hands. The keys to survival are selection and serving size, and you need quick, reliable data to come out on top in both arenas. In short, *Fast Food Facts* can be your guide.

What's Good About Fast Food?

Fast food is a distinctly American part of the food service business; however, it's an aspect of American life that is growing outside of the United States every day. It's unusual today to travel to any country in the world and not find fast-food restaurants. Quickness and convenience are winning over even the harshest critics of the American fast-food phenomenon. And whether you're in Pittsburgh or Paris, your favorite fast-food restaurant is likely to be serving up familiar fare.

Studies of the leading chains show remarkable uniformity in the portion size and the nutritional value of specific menu items. Regardless of the restaurant's location, you can assume that the fat and calories in any individual menu item are going to be the same. Foods at fast-food restaurants also are fresh and safe to consume. Food safety and cleanliness guidelines are stringent, and each individual restaurant is required to meet them.

Food selection at fast-food restaurants is constantly improving as well. Many now offer salad bars, grilled or baked meat or fish, baked potatoes, and healthy soups. Diet soft drinks and reduced-fat milk also are readily available. However, all of these health-conscious options are only helpful if you choose one of them. The decision is yours.

Smart Choices, Smart Meals

For most people an occasional fast-food meal will not upset an otherwise healthy diet and lifestyle. What you order and how often you order it are the real issues. If you eat at fast-food restaurants every day, you need to be very careful about your food choices. Select only Smart Choices, which are indicated in the food lists in this book by the symbol ☀. (The guidelines we used for designating Smart Choices appear on page 14.) If you only occasionally eat at fast-food restaurants, the individual choices you make are not as crucial. However moderation, as always, is important.

Look for meals that meet the following guidelines. If sodium is a concern, keep to a limit of 1000 milligrams or less for any fast-food meal.

Men	Women
700-900 calories	500-700 calories
30-35 fat grams	20-25 fat grams

To give you ideas for choosing menu items that add up to a nutritious and healthful fast-food meal, we've created Smart Meals. These meal menus appear at the end of most restaurant listings in the book. The guidelines we used for creating Smart Meals appear on page 15.

Good nutrition can be assured, even when fast food is part of your lifestyle, by eating a variety of foods every day, including vegetables and fruits, low-fat dairy products, and whole-grain breads and cereals. For added assurance when restaurant choices are limited, you can supplement a fast-food meal with fruit or vegetables from home. To make sure you're getting the nutrients you need every day, whether fast food is part of your diet or not, take the Nutrition Quotient Quiz.

Nutrition Quotient Quiz

Answer the questions based on your food intake for one day, then read the evaluations that follow. Put a check by the evaluation that best describes your responses.

Yes   *No*

☐   ☐   Did I eat a total of five servings of fruits and/or vegetables?

☐   ☐   Did I eat two or three servings of low-fat dairy foods such as skim or low-fat milk, nonfat or low-fat yogurt, or low-fat cheese?

☐   ☐   For men: Did I eat 7 ounces or less of meat, poultry, and fish?

☐   ☐   For women: Did I eat 5 ounces or less of meat, poultry, and fish?

☐   ☐   Were most of my grain choices whole-grain rather than refined?

☐   ☐   Did I limit my intake of foods that contain added sugars and fats?

☐   ☐   And although not a food choice, did I accumulate 30 minutes of physical activity?

If you answered "yes" to all of the questions, your nutrition quotient is excellent, and you don't need to worry about incorporating fast food into your diet.

If you can answer "yes" to the majority of the questions for most days over a period of one week, your nutrition quotient is very good. You too can be comfortable about fitting fast food into your life, but you should stick to Smart Choices whenever possible.

If you're like many people and answered "no" to most of the questions, you need to become more conscious of the food choices you make – especially the fast-food choices.

Making the Best Fast-food Choices

Whether eating out or at home, all of us should try to eat a variety of foods in moderate portions and to consume no more than one-third of our daily calories from fat. Consider these suggestions when making your own smart choices.

Burgers—Single, no sauce

Set your sights on a single-patty burger, if you want to keep the fat and calories to a minimum. Even two regular, plain hamburgers usually have less fat than a double burger with cheese and special sauces. So if you've got a double-decker appetite, skip the usual dressings and pile on the lettuce and tomatoes instead.

Chicken and fish—Beware the breading

Battering, breading, or deep-frying cancels out the normal, low-fat advantages of chicken and fish. Choose roasted, grilled, or broiled fish or chicken without breading and cooked without fat. If fried chicken or fish are your only choices, choose regular coating over extra crispy. Even better, remove the batter to reduce the calories and eliminate most of the fat and sodium.

Sandwiches—Many low-fat options

A sandwich can be a very good choice at a fast-food restaurant. Choose a regular- or junior-size version of a roast beef, ham-and-cheese, or turkey sandwich. Even with barbecue sauce, a roast beef sandwich will provide fewer calories and fat than a hamburger. Croissant sandwiches are deceptively high in fat. Stick with regular or whole-grain bread, a bun, pita bread, or a tortilla.

Pizza—Extra toppings, extra calories

As a snack or a quick meal, pizza fits nicely into a well-balanced diet. Choose thin-crust pizza instead of thick-crust or deep-dish pizza. When choosing toppings, stay with mushrooms, onions, green or hot peppers, and other vegetable toppings. Extra cheese, pepperoni, and sausage mean extra fat and calories. To avoid extra sodium, skip the olives and anchovies.

Potatoes—Plain and baked are best

Potatoes are nourishing, filling, and virtually free of fat and sodium. But all of this goodness goes awry when toppings such as cheese sauce, crumbled bacon, or sour cream are added. Have a baked potato topped with a low-fat protein (one-quarter cup of cottage cheese or one to two tablespoons of grated Swiss, cheddar, or parmesan cheese) and a salad for a complete, satisfying, and healthy meal. Go easy on the French fries if you are trying to cut calories.

Southwestern fare—Stay free of fried

Entrees made with soft flour tortillas are generally better choices than those made with fried (hard) corn tortillas. Choose chicken, bean, or beef burritos or other non-fried items, and spice them to your taste. To keep the fat and calories down, skip the guacamole and sour cream and pile on extra salsa, tomatoes, and lettuce. Chili is a surprisingly good choice as well; even a large bowl has only 300 calories and 12 grams of fat.

Salad—A healthy choice

A trip to the salad bar is a healthy alternative to high-fat fast food. Rely on raw vegetables and pass on the prepared salads, such as potato salad and pasta salad. Some pre-made salads are good choices, such as grilled chicken or garden salads. Avoid taco salads, Caesar salads, and chef salads, which include meats, cheeses, and eggs that boost the fat content. As always, stick with low-calorie, reduced-fat, or nonfat salad dressings.

Beverages—Watch for hidden sugar and fat

The most popular beverages at fast-food restaurants are shakes and soft drinks. Better choices are diet beverages, reduced-fat or skim milk, fruit juice, or—the best of all beverage choices—water. Coffee and tea are good choices as well.

Dessert—The simpler the better

Low-fat or nonfat frozen yogurt cones can satisfy your sweet tooth with little damage.

You can also satisfy your dessert craving by bringing fresh fruit from home. Try eating your "dessert" fruit first; it's a creative way to curb your appetite and avoid overeating.

Breakfast—Proceed with caution

As with fast-food desserts, simpler is better when it comes to fast-food breakfasts. Breakfast sandwiches, especially sausage versions, are very high in fat and calories. Start your day with low-fat muffins, English muffins, bagels, or toast instead. Add one scrambled egg, fruit juice, and reduced-fat or skim milk. Pancakes without butter are a surprisingly good breakfast option as well.

Since many of us are eating fast food quite frequently, it's important that we learn how to do it healthfully. The following chart summarizes some options that you may face in any given restaurant. The left-hand column gives the recommended choice.

Choose . . .	**Instead of . . .**
Regular Hamburger	Double Burger with Sauce
270 calories	825 calories
9 grams fat	42 grams fat
BBQ Chicken Sandwich	Deep-fried Breaded Chicken Sandwich
310 calories	710 calories
6 grams fat	43 grams fat
Roasted Chicken Breast	Extra Crispy Chicken Breast
170 calories	500 calories
5 grams fat	35 grams fat
Baked Fish Sandwich	Deep-fried Breaded Fish Sandwich
290 calories	700 calories
2 grams fat	41 grams fat
Turkey Wrap Sandwich	Tuna Wrap Sandwich
550 calories	950 calories
12 grams fat	64 grams fat
Junior Roast Beef Sandwich	Giant Roast Beef Sandwich
324 calories	555 calories
14 grams fat	28 grams fat
Thin-crust Cheese Pizza (2 slices)	Deep-dish Cheese Pizza (2 slices)
255 calories	465 calories
11 grams fat	20 grams fat

Choose ...	**Instead of ...**
Baked Potato	Deluxe Baked Potato (with toppings)
355 calories	750 calories
0 grams fat	35 grams fat
Mashed Potatoes and Gravy	Medium French Fries
120 calories	380 calories
6 grams fat	19 grams fat
Steak Soft Taco	Seven-layer Burrito
200 calories	540 calories
7 grams fat	24 grams fat
Grilled Chicken Salad	Taco Salad
240 calories	840 calories
11 grams fat	52 grams fat
Orange Juice (6 ounces)	Chocolate Shake (14 ounces)
80 calories	560 calories
0 grams fat	15 grams fat
Regular Yogurt Cone	Heath Blizzard®
180 calories	820 calories
less than 1 gram fat	33 grams fat
Low-fat Triple Berry Muffin	Pecan Roll
270 calories	900 calories
3 grams fat	48 grams fat
Pancakes with Syrup	Big Country® Sausage Breakfast
490 calories	1000 calories
7 grams fat	66 grams fat

Fast-food Tips

As you think about fitting fast food into your healthy lifestyle, remember that eating three meals a day is just as important as making healthy food choices. It's tempting to skip breakfast or lunch when you're dieting to lose weight, or when life gets too hectic. This can lead to overeating when you finally do eat, and if you're eating fast food—well, you can imagine where that can lead. The following tips will help you make the right fast-food choices for you.

Eat mainly at meal times. The average calorie content of a fast-food meal is 685, which is reasonable for many people. However, when you eat fast-food items (such as French fries) as snacks rather than as meals, you can add a hefty average of 427 calories to your usual daily intake. This can easily put you well over your daily calorie limit.

Buy small. Avoid menu choices labeled "jumbo," "giant," or "deluxe." Larger servings mean extra calories and usually more fat, cholesterol, and sodium as well.

Limit high-fat condiments. Each tablespoon of salad dressing, mayonnaise, mayonnaise-based dressing, or another fat-containing sauce adds an extra 100 to 200 calories to a sandwich or salad. If no low-fat versions are available, take just a small amount of the regular condiment. You may find that a little goes a long way and that food tastes even better when it's not smothered in add-ons.

Share. French fries, a large sandwich, or dessert will taste even better when shared with a friend. Or take half home for another meal.

About This Edition

The information in the food lists is presented in four parts or groups:

1) Menu items;

2) Serving sizes and calories;

3) Nutrients in each serving, including grams of fat, grams of saturated fat, milligrams of sodium, grams of protein, and grams of carbohydrate; and

4) Carbohydrate choices and exchange choices.

The information for each menu item stretches across two pages of the open book. The first two parts—often the most used—appear on the left-hand page. The second two parts are on the right-hand page. The exchange and carbohydrate choices—essential information for people following a meal plan for weight loss or for other health reasons—are conveniently located to the far right.

Carbohydrate choices were calculated using the 15-gram equation. Because fiber is a carbohydrate that is not digested, fiber was subtracted from the total grams of carbohydrate before calculating the carbohydrate and exchange choices for items with five or more grams of fiber.

The 15-gram Equation
15 grams of carbohydrate = 1 carbohydrate choice

Exchange choices are based on the *Exchange Lists* published by the American Diabetes Association and The American Dietetic Association. Exchanges include starch; fruit; milk; other carbohydrates; vegetable; very lean, lean, medium fat, or high fat meat; and fat. Some of the nutrient values for food items are based on actual laboratory analysis, and some were calculated from nutrient composition tables. The values listed are averages and may vary from restaurant to restaurant.

☀ Smart Choices are the most healthful menu items offered by each restaurant. They are designated in the lists by a small light bulb in the left margin. The following guidelines were used to determine Smart Choices:

- Entrees (main dishes, main-dish soups and salads, sandwiches): Less than 700 calories; no high fat meat or fat exchanges

- Side orders (vegetables, bread, side soups, salads, salad dressings): 0 to 1 fat exchanges

- Salad bar selections and condiments: Less than 3 grams of fat

- Beverages: Skim or reduced-fat milk or fruit juice
- Desserts: Less than 250 calories; 0 to 1 fat exchanges

SMART MEALS

Smart Meals are menus that appear at the end of most restaurant sections. We used the following guidelines to create Smart Meals:

- Each Smart Meal includes foods from at least three food groups (grains, dairy, vegetables, fruit, or meat).
- A Smart Meal has 700 calories or less and 20 grams or less of fat.
- All menu items selected for Smart Meals are Smart Choices or free foods. (Free foods are foods with less than 20 calories per serving.)

This book is designed to alert you to the nutritive values, carbohydrate choices, and exchange choices for food items and to help you make smart fast-food choices. You can enjoy the taste and convenience of eating at fast-food restaurants and still eat healthfully.

Nutrition Information for 20 Popular Fast-Food Restaurants

MENU ITEM	SERVING SIZE	CALORIES	CALORIES FROM FAT
ARBY'S			
ROAST BEEF SANDWICHES			
Arby's Melt with Cheddar Sandwich	1 (5.2 oz)	368	162
Arby-Q Sandwich	1 (6.4 oz)	431	162
Bac'n Cheddar Deluxe Sandwich	1 (8.1 oz)	539	306
Beef 'n Cheddar Sandwich	1 (6.7 oz)	487	252
Giant Roast Beef Sandwich	1 (8.1 oz)	555	252
Junior Roast Beef Sandwich	1 (4.4 oz)	324	126
🔆 Regular Roast Beef Sandwich	1 (5.4 oz)	388	171
Super Roast Beef Sandwich	1 (8.7 oz)	523	243
CHICKEN			
Breaded Chicken Fillet	1 (7.2 oz)	536	252
Chicken Cordon Bleu Sandwich	1 (8.5 oz)	623	297
Chicken Fingers	2 pieces (3.6 oz)	290	144
🔆 Grilled Chicken BBQ Sandwich	1 (7.1 oz)	388	117
Grilled Chicken Deluxe Sandwich	1 (8.1 oz)	430	180
Roast Chicken Club Sandwich	1 (8.5 oz)	546	279
Roast Chicken Deluxe Sandwich	1 (7.6 oz)	433	198
🔆 Roast Chicken Santa Fe Sandwich	1 (6.4 oz)	436	198
SUB ROLL SANDWICHES			
🔆 French Dip Sandwich	1 (6.8 oz)	475	198
🔆 Hot Ham 'n Swiss Sandwich	1 (9.3 oz)	500	207
Italian Sandwich	1 (10.1 oz)	675	324
Philly Beef 'n Swiss Sandwich	1 (10.4 oz)	755	423

🔆 Smart Choice

TOTAL FAT (g)	SATURATED FAT (g)	SODIUM (mg)	PROTEIN (g)	CARBOHYDRATE (g)	CARBOHYDRATE CHOICES	EXCHANGES
18	6	937	18	36	2½	2½ starch, 2 med. fat meat, 1 fat
18	6	1321	22	48	3	3 starch, 2 med. fat meat, 1 fat
34	10	1140	22	38	2½	2½ starch, 2½ med. fat meat, 4 fat
28	9	1216	25	40	2½	2½ starch, 3 med. fat meat, 2 fat
28	11	1561	35	38*	2½	2½ starch, 4 med. fat meat, 1 fat
14	5	779	17	35	2	2 starch, 2 med. fat meat, 1 fat
19	7	1009	23	33	2	2 starch, 3 med. fat meat
27	9	1189	25	45*	3	3 starch, 3 med. fat meat, 2 fat
28	5	1016	28	41*	3	3 starch, 3 med. fat meat, 2 fat
33	8	1594	38	41*	3	3 starch, 4 med. fat meat, 2 fat
16	2	677	16	20	1	1 starch, 2 med. fat meat, 1 fat
13	3	1002	23	47	3	3 starch, 2½ med. fat meat
20	4	848	23	41	3	3 starch, 2½ med. fat meat, 1 fat
31	9	1103	31	37	2½	2½ starch, 3½ med. fat meat, 2 fat
22	5	763	24	36	2½	2½ starch, 2½ med. fat meat, 1 fat
22	6	818	29	35	2½	2½ starch, 3½ med. fat meat
22	8	1411	30	40	2½	2½ starch, 4 med. fat meat
23	7	1664	30	43	3	3 starch, 4 med. fat meat
36	13	2089	30	46	3	3 starch, 4 med. fat meat, 3 fat
47	15	2025	39	48	3	3 starch, 5 med. fat meat, 4 fat

1 Carbohydrate Choice = 1 starch or 1 fruit or 1 milk exchange
* Grams of fiber subtracted from total carbohydrate

MENU ITEM	SERVING SIZE	CALORIES	CALORIES FROM FAT
Roast Beef Sandwich	1 (10.8 oz)	700	378
Triple Cheese Melt Sandwich	1 (8.4 oz)	720	405
Turkey Sandwich	1 (9.8 oz)	550	243
LIGHT MENU SANDWICHES			
☼ Roast Beef Deluxe Sandwich	1 (6.4 oz)	296	90
☼ Roast Chicken Deluxe Sandwich	1 (6.8 oz)	276	54
☼ Roast Turkey Deluxe Sandwich	1 (6.8 oz)	260	63
OTHER SANDWICHES			
Fish Fillet Sandwich	1 (7.7 oz)	529	243
☼ Ham 'n Cheese Sandwich	1 (5.9 oz)	359	126
☼ Ham 'n Cheese Melt Sandwich	1 (4.9 oz)	329	117
BAKED POTATOES			
☼ Baked Potato, plain	1 (11.5 oz)	355	3
Baked Potato with Margarine & Sour Cream	1 (14 oz)	578	216
Broccoli 'n Cheddar Baked Potato	1 (15.7 oz)	571	180
Deluxe Baked Potato	1 (15.3 oz)	736	324
SIDE ORDERS			
Cheddar Curly Fries	1 order (4.25 oz)	333	163
Curly Fries	1 order (3.5 oz)	300	135
French Fries	1 order (2.5 oz)	246	117
Potato Cakes (2)	1 order (3 oz)	204	108
SOUPS			
☼ Boston Clam Chowder Soup	8 oz	190	81

☼ Smart Choice

TOTAL FAT (g)	SATURATED FAT (g)	SODIUM (mg)	PROTEIN (g)	CARBOHYDRATE (g)	CARBOHYDRATE CHOICES	EXCHANGES
42	14	2034	38	44	3	3 starch, 5 med. fat meat, 3 fat
45	16	1797	37	46	3	3 starch, 5 med. fat meat, 4 fat
27	7	2084	31	47	3	3 starch, 4 med. fat meat, 1 fat
10	3	826	18	27*	2	2 starch, 2 med. fat meat
6	2	777	20	33	2	2 starch, 2 lean meat
7	2	1262	20	33	2	2 starch, 2 lean meat
27	7	864	23	50	3	3 starch, 3 med. fat meat, 2 fat
14	5	1283	24	34	2	2 starch, 3 med. fat meat
13	4	1013	20	34	2	2 starch, 2½ med. fat meat
0	0	26	7	75*	5	5 starch
24	9	209	9	78*	5	5 starch, 4 fat
20	5	565	14	80*	5	5 starch, 1 med. fat meat, 2 fat
36	16	499	19	79*	5	5 starch, 2 med. fat meat, 4 fat
18	4	1016	5	40	2½	2½ starch, 3 fat
15	3	853	4	38	2½	2½ starch, 3 fat
13	3	114	2	30	2	2 starch, 2 fat
12	2	397	2	20	1	1½ starch, 2 fat
9	3	965	9	18	1	1 starch, 1 med. fat meat, 1 fat

1 Carbohydrate Choice = 1 starch or 1 fruit or 1 milk exchange
* Grams of fiber subtracted from total carbohydrate

MENU ITEM	SERVING SIZE	CALORIES	CALORIES FROM FAT
☀ Cream of Broccoli Soup	8 oz	160	72
☀ Lumberjack Mixed Vegetable Soup	8 oz	90	36
☀ Old Fashion Chicken Noodle Soup	8 oz	80	18
☀ Potato with Bacon Soup	8 oz	170	63
☀ Timberline Chili Soup	8 oz	220	90
Wisconsin Cheese Soup	8 oz	280	162
SALADS			
☀ Garden Salad	1 (11.9 oz)	61	3
☀ Roast Chicken Salad	1 (14.4 oz)	149	18
☀ Side Salad	1 (5 oz)	23	3
SALAD DRESSINGS			
Blue Cheese Salad Dressing	2 oz	290	279
☀ Buttermilk Ranch Salad Dressing, Reduced Calorie	2 oz	50	0
Honey French Salad Dressing	2 oz	280	207
☀ Italian Salad Dressing, Reduced Calorie	2 oz	20	9
☀ Red Ranch Salad Dressing	0.5 oz	75	54
Thousand Island Salad Dressing	2 oz	260	234
CONDIMENTS			
☀ Arby's Sauce	0.5 oz	15	2
☀ Barbeque Sauce	0.5 oz	30	0
☀ Beef Stock Au Jus	2 oz	10	0
Cheddar Cheese Sauce	0.75 oz	35	27

☀ Smart Choice

TOTAL FAT (g)	SATURATED FAT (g)	SODIUM (mg)	PROTEIN (g)	CARBOHYDRATE (g)	CARBOHYDRATE CHOICES	EXCHANGES
8	4	1005	7	15	1	1 starch, 1 high fat meat
4	2	1150	2	10	½	½ starch, 1 fat or 2 veg, 1 fat
2	0	850	6	11	1	1 starch
7	3	905	6	23	1½	1½ starch, 1 fat
10	4	1130	18	10*	1	1 starch, 2 med. fat meat
18	7	1065	10	20	1	1 starch, 1 high fat meat, 2 fat
1	0	40	3	7*	½	2 veg
2	<1	418	20	7*	½	2 veg, 3 very lean meat
0	0	15	1	4	0	1 veg
31	6	580	2	2	0	6 fat
0	0	710	0	12	1	1 other carb
23	3	400	0	18	1	1 other carb, 4 fat
1	0	1000	0	3	0	free
6	1	115	0	5	0	1 fat
26	4	420	0	7	½	½ other carb, 5 fat
0	0	113	0	4	0	free
0	0	185	0	7	½	½ other carb
0	0	440	0	1	0	free
3	1	139	1	1	0	½ fat

1 Carbohydrate Choice = 1 starch or 1 fruit or 1 milk exchange
* Grams of fiber subtracted from total carbohydrate

MENU ITEM	SERVING SIZE	CALORIES	CALORIES FROM FAT
Honey Mayonnaise, Reduced Calorie	0.5 oz	70	63
Horsey Sauce	0.5 oz	60	45
Italian Sub Sauce	0.5 oz	70	63
☀ Ketchup	0.5 oz	16	0
Mayonnaise	0.5 oz	110	108
☀ Mayonnaise, Light Cholesterol Free	0.25 oz	12	9
☀ Mustard, German Style	0.16 oz	5	0
Parmesan Cheese Sauce	0.5 oz	70	63
☀ Table Syrup	1 oz	100	0
Tartar Sauce	1 oz	140	135

DESSERTS

Apple Turnover	1 (3.2 oz)	330	126
Cheesecake, plain	1 (3 oz)	320	207
Cherry Turnover	1 (3.2 oz)	320	117
☀ Chocolate Chip Cookie	1 (1 oz)	125	54
Polar Swirl, Butterfinger	1 (11.6 oz)	457	162
Polar Swirl, Heath	1 (11.6 oz)	543	198
Polar Swirl, Oreo	1 (11.6 oz)	482	198
Polar Swirl, Peanut Butter Cup	1 (11.6 oz)	517	216
Polar Swirl, Snickers	1 (11.6 oz)	511	171

SHAKES

Chocolate Shake	12 oz	451	108
Jamocha Shake	12 oz	384	90
Vanilla Shake	12 oz	360	108

☀ Smart Choice

TOTAL FAT (g)	SATURATED FAT (g)	SODIUM (mg)	PROTEIN (g)	CARBOHYDRATE (g)	CARBOHYDRATE CHOICES	EXCHANGES
7	1	135	0	1	0	1 fat
5	1	150	0	2	0	1 fat
7	1	240	0	1	0	1 fat
0	0	143	0	4	0	free
12	7	80	0	0	0	2 fat
1	0	64	0	0.5	0	free
0	0	70	0	1	0	free
7	1	130	1	2	0	1 fat
0	0	30	0	25	1½	1½ other carb
15	2	220	0	0	0	3 fat
14	7	180	4	48	3	3 other carb, 2 fat
23	14	240	5	23	1½	1½ other carb, 4½ fat
13	5	190	4	46	3	3 other carb, 2 fat
6	2	85	2	16	1	1 other carb, 1 fat
18	8	318	15	62	4	4 other carb, 3 fat
22	5	346	15	76	5	5 other carb, 4 fat
22	10	521	15	66	4	4 other carb, 4 fat
24	8	385	20	61	4	4 other carb, 5 fat
19	7	351	15	73	5	5 other carb, 3 fat
12	3	341	15	76	5	5 other carb, 2 fat
10	3	262	15	62	4	4 other carb, 2 fat
12	4	281	15	50	3	3 other carb, 2 fat

1 Carbohydrate Choice = 1 starch or 1 fruit or 1 milk exchange
* Grams of fiber subtracted from total carbohydrate

MENU ITEM	SERVING SIZE	CALORIES	CALORIES FROM FAT
SOFT DRINKS			
Coca-Cola Classic®	12 oz	140	0
Diet Coke®	12 oz	0	0
Diet Pepsi®	12 oz	0	0
Diet 7 Up®	12 oz	0	0
Dr. Pepper®	12 oz	160	0
Nehi Orange®	12 oz	195	0
Pepsi Cola®	12 oz	150	0
RC Cola®	12 oz	165	0
RC Diet Rite®	12 oz	1	0
7 Up®	12 oz	144	0
Upper Ten®	12 oz	169	0
OTHER BEVERAGES			
Coffee, black	8 oz	3	0
Hot Chocolate	8 oz	110	9
Iced Tea	16 oz	6	0
☀ Orange Juice	6 oz	82	0
BREAKFAST			
Bacon (2 pieces)	1 order (0.53 oz)	90	63
Biscuit, plain	1 (2.9 oz)	280	135
Blueberry Muffin	1 (2.3 oz)	230	81
Cinnamon Nut Danish	1 (3.5 oz)	360	99
Croissant, plain	1 (2 oz)	220	108
Egg Portion	1 (1.6 oz)	95	72

 Smart Choice

TOTAL FAT (g)	SATURATED FAT (g)	SODIUM (mg)	PROTEIN (g)	CARBOHYDRATE (g)	CARBOHYDRATE CHOICES	EXCHANGES
0	0	50	0	39	2½	2½ other carb
0	0	40	0	0	0	free
0	0	35	0	0	0	free
0	0	35	0	0	0	free
0	0	55	0	40	3½	3½ other carb
0	0	52	0	52	3½	3½ other carb
0	0	35	0	41	3	3 other carb
0	0	52	0	43	3	3 other carb
0	0	10	0	0	0	free
0	0	34	0	38	2½	2½ other carb
0	0	40	0	42	3	3 other carb
0	0	3	0	0	0	free
1	<1	120	2	23	1½	1½ other carb
0	0	12	0	1	0	free
0	0	2	0	20	1	1 fruit
7	3	220	5	0	0	1½ fat
15	3	730	6	34	2	2 starch, 3 fat
9	2	290	2	35	2	2 starch, 2 fat
11	1	105	6	60	4	4 starch, 2 fat
12	7	230	4	25	1½	1½ starch, 2 fat
8	2	54	0.5	0.5	0	1½ fat

1 Carbohydrate Choice = 1 starch or 1 fruit or 1 milk exchange
* Grams of fiber subtracted from total carbohydrate

MENU ITEM	SERVING SIZE	CALORIES	CALORIES FROM FAT
French-Toastix	6 (4.4 oz)	430	189
☀ Ham	1 order (1.5 oz)	45	9
Sausage	1 order (1.3 oz)	163	135

SMART MEAL, ARBY'S

Regular Roast Beef Sandwich	**Calories:**	437
Side Salad	**Fat:**	20 grams
Italian Salad Dressing,	**Carb Choices:**	2½
Reduced Calorie (2 oz)	**Exchanges:**	2 starch, 1 veg,
Iced Tea (unsweetened)		3 med. fat meat

Roast Chicken Salad	**Calories:**	259
Italian Salad Dressing,	**Fat:**	7 grams
Reduced Calorie (2 oz)	**Carb Choices:**	1½
Lumberjack Mixed Vegetable Soup	**Exchanges:**	1 starch, 1 veg,
		3 very lean meat,
		1 fat

TOTAL FAT (g)	SATURATED FAT (g)	SODIUM (mg)	PROTEIN (g)	CARBOHYDRATE (g)	CARBOHYDRATE CHOICES	EXCHANGES
21	5	550	10	52	3½	3½ starch, 4 fat
1	<1	405	7	0	0	1 very lean meat
15	6	321	7	0	0	1 med. fat meat, 2 fat

SMART MEAL, ARBY'S

Roast Turkey Deluxe Light Menu Sandwich	**Calories:**	371
Garden Salad	**Fat:**	8 grams
Buttermilk Ranch Salad Dressing,	**Carb Choices:**	3½
Reduced Calorie (2 oz)	**Exchanges:**	2 starch,
Diet Soft Drink		1 other carb,
		1 veg,
		2 lean meat

1 Carbohydrate Choice = 1 starch or 1 fruit or 1 milk exchange
* Grams of fiber subtracted from total carbohydrate

MENU ITEM	SERVING SIZE	CALORIES	CALORIES FROM FAT
BLIMPIE			
SUBS			
💡 Blimpie® Best Sub, 6-inch	1	410	120
Cheese Trio Sub, 6-inch	1	510	200
💡 Club Sub, 6-inch	1	450	120
Five Meatball Sub, 6-inch	1	500	200
💡 Grilled Chicken Sub, 6-inch	1	400	80
💡 Ham & Swiss Sub, 6-inch	1	400	120
Ham, Salami, Provolone Sub, 6-inch	1	590	250
💡 Roast Beef Sub, 6-inch	1	340	40
Steak & Cheese Sub, 6-inch	1	550	230
Tuna Sub, 6-inch	1	570	290
💡 Turkey Sub, 6-inch	1	320	40
CHICKEN			
Chicken Fajita	1 (9.8 oz)	420	140
💡 Grilled Chicken Salad (without dressing)	1 (16.3 oz)	350	110
CONDIMENTS			
💡 Salsa	.75 oz	5	0

💡 Smart Choice

TOTAL FAT (g)	SATURATED FAT (g)	SODIUM (mg)	PROTEIN (g)	CARBOHYDRATE (g)	CARBOHYDRATE CHOICES	EXCHANGES
13	5	1480	26	47	3	3 starch, 2½ med. fat meat
23	13	1060	26	51	3½	3½ starch, 2 med. fat meat, 2 fat
13	6	1350	30	53	3½	3½ starch, 3 med. fat meat
22	8	970	23	52	3½	3½ starch, 2 med. fat meat, 2 fat
9	2	950	28	52	3½	3½ starch, 2½ lean meat
13	7	970	25	47	3	3 starch, 2½ med. fat meat
28	11	1880	32	52	3½	3½ starch, 3½ med. fat meat, 1½ fat
5	1	870	27	42*	3	3 starch, 3 very lean meat
26	4	1080	27	51	3½	3½ starch, 3 med. fat meat, 2 fat
32	5	790	21	50	3	3 starch, 1½ med. fat meat, 4 fat
5	1	890	19	51	3½	3½ starch, 2 lean meat
16	6	520	21	48	3	3 starch, 2 med. fat meat, 1 fat
12	0	1190	47	13	1	1 starch, 6 lean meat
0	0	210	0	1	0	free

1 Carbohydrate Choice = 1 starch or 1 fruit or 1 milk exchange
* Grams of fiber subtracted from total carbohydrate

MENU ITEM	SERVING SIZE	CALORIES	CALORIES FROM FAT
BOSTON MARKET			
ENTREES			
Chicken (with skin)	½ chicken (10 oz)	630	330
☀ Chicken, Dark Meat (without skin)	¼ chicken (3.7 oz)	210	90
☀ Chicken, Dark Meat (with skin)	¼ chicken (4.7 oz)	330	200
☀ Chicken, White Meat (with skin)	¼ chicken (5.4 oz)	330	150
☀ Chicken, White Meat (without skin or wing)	¼ chicken (3.7 oz)	160	35
Chunky Chicken Salad	¾ cup (5.5 oz)	370	240
☀ Ham with Cinnamon Apples	1 order (8 oz)	350	110
☀ Meat Loaf & Brown Gravy	1 order (7 oz)	390	200
☀ Meat Loaf & Chunky Tomato Sauce	1 order (8 oz)	370	160
Original Chicken Pot Pie	1 pie (15 oz)	750	300
☀ Skinless Rotisserie Turkey Breast	1 order (5 oz)	170	10
SANDWICHES			
☀ Chicken Sandwich (no cheese or sauce)	1 (11.5 oz)	430	40
Chicken Sandwich (with cheese and sauce)	1 (12 oz)	750	300
☀ Chicken Salad Sandwich	1 (11.5 oz)	680	270
☀ Ham Sandwich (no cheese or sauce)	1 (9.5 oz)	450	80
Ham Sandwich (with cheese and sauce)	1 (11.5 oz)	760	320

☀ Smart Choice

TOTAL FAT (g)	SATURATED FAT (g)	SODIUM (mg)	PROTEIN (g)	CARBOHYDRATE (g)	CARBOHYDRATE CHOICES	EXCHANGES
37	10	960	74	2	0	11 lean meat
10	3	320	28	1	0	4 lean meat
22	6	460	31	2	0	4½ med. fat meat
17	5	530	43	2	0	6 lean meat
4	1	350	31	0	0	4 very lean meat
27	5	800	28	3	0	4 med. fat meat, 1 fat
13	5	1750	25	35	2	2 other carb, 3 med. fat meat
22	8	1040	30	19	1	1 starch, 4 med. fat meat
18	8	1170	30	22	1½	1½ starch, 4 med. fat meat
34	9	2380	34	72*	5	5 starch, 3 med. fat meat, 3 fat
1	<1	850	36	1	0	5 very lean meat
5	1	910	34	57*	4	4 starch, 4 very lean meat
33	12	1860	41	67*	5	5 starch, 4½ med. fat meat, 1 fat
30	5	1360	39	63	4	4 starch, 5 med. fat meat
9	3	1600	25	66	4	4 starch, 3 lean meat
35	13	1880	38	71	5	5 starch, 4 med. fat meat, 2 fat

1 Carbohydrate Choice = 1 starch or 1 fruit or 1 milk exchange
* Grams of fiber subtracted from total carbohydrate

MENU ITEM	SERVING SIZE	CALORIES	CALORIES FROM FAT
💡 Ham & Turkey Club Sandwich (no cheese or sauce)	1 (9.5 oz)	430	60
Ham & Turkey Club Sandwich (with cheese and sauce)	1 (13.5 oz)	890	400
💡 Meat Loaf Sandwich (no cheese)	1 (12.5 oz)	690	190
Meat Loaf Sandwich (with cheese)	1 (13.5 oz)	860	290
💡 Turkey Sandwich (no cheese or sauce)	1 (9.5 oz)	400	30
Turkey Sandwich (with cheese and sauce)	1 (11.5 oz)	710	260
HOT SIDE DISHES			
BBQ Baked Beans	¾ cup	330	80
💡 Butternut Squash	¾ cup	160	60
💡 Chicken Gravy	1 (1 oz)	15	10
Creamed Spinach	¾ cup	280	190
💡 Green Bean Casserole	¾ cup	90	40
Homestyle Mashed Potatoes & Gravy	¾ cup	200	80
💡 Hot Cinnamon Apples	¾ cup	250	40
Macaroni & Cheese	¾ cup	280	90
Mashed Potatoes	⅔ cup	180	80
💡 New Potatoes	¾ cup	130	20
💡 Rice Pilaf	⅔ cup	180	45
💡 Steamed Vegetables	⅔ cup	35	5
Stuffing	¾ cup	310	110
💡 Whole Kernel Corn	¾ cup	180	40
💡 Zucchini Marinara	¾ cup	80	40

💡 Smart Choice

TOTAL FAT (g)	SATURATED FAT (g)	SODIUM (mg)	PROTEIN (g)	CARBOHYDRATE (g)	CARBOHYDRATE CHOICES	EXCHANGES
6	2	1330	29	64	4	4 starch, 3 lean meat
44	20	2350	48	76	5	5 starch, 5 med. fat meat, 2 fat
21	7	1610	40	80*	5	5 starch, 4 med. fat meat
33	16	2270	46	89*	6	6 starch, 5 med. fat meat
4	1	1070	32	61	4	4 starch, 4 very lean meat
28	10	1390	45	68	4½	4½ starch, 5 med. fat meat
9	3	630	11	44*	3	3 starch, 2 fat
6	4	580	2	25	1½	1½ starch, 1 fat
1	0	170	0	2	0	free
21	13	820	9	12	1	3 veg or 1 starch, 1 med. fat meat, 3 fat
5	2	580	2	10	½	2 veg, 1 fat
9	5	560	3	27	2	2 starch, 1½ fat
5	<1	45	0	56	4	4 fruit, 1 fat
10	6	760	12	36	2½	2½ starch, 1 high fat meat
8	5	390	3	25	1½	1½ starch, 1½ fat
3	0	150	3	25	1½	1½ starch
5	1	600	5	32	2	2 starch, 1 fat
1	0	35	2	7	½	1 veg
12	2	1140	6	44	3	3 starch, 2 fat
4	<1	170	5	30	2	2 starch, 1 fat
4	<1	470	2	10	½	2 veg, 1 fat

1 Carbohydrate Choice = 1 starch or 1 fruit or 1 milk exchange
* Grams of fiber subtracted from total carbohydrate

MENU ITEM	SERVING SIZE	CALORIES	CALORIES FROM FAT
COLD SIDE DISHES			
Caesar Side Salad	1 (4 oz)	210	150
Cole Slaw	¾ cup	280	140
☼ Corn Bread, small loaf	1	200	50
☼ Cranberry Relish	¾ cup	370	45
☼ Fruit Salad	¾ cup	70	5
☼ Honey Wheat Roll	½ roll	150	10
Mediterranean Pasta Salad	¾ cup	170	90
Tortellini Salad	¾ cup	380	220
SOUPS			
☼ Chicken Soup	¾ cup	80	25
☼ Chicken Tortilla Soup	1 cup	220	100
SALADS			
Caesar Salad Entree	1 (10 oz)	520	390
☼ Caesar Salad without Dressing	1 (8 oz)	240	120
Chicken Caesar Salad	1 (13 oz)	670	420
DESSERTS			
Brownie	1	450	240
Chocolate Chip Cookie	1	340	150

☼ Smart Choice

TOTAL FAT (g)	SATURATED FAT (g)	SODIUM (mg)	PROTEIN (g)	CARBOHYDRATE (g)	CARBOHYDRATE CHOICES	EXCHANGES
17	5	560	8	6	0	1 veg, 1 med. fat meat, 2 fat
16	3	520	2	32	2	2 starch, 3 fat
6	2	390	3	33	2	2 starch, 1 fat
5	<1	5	2	79*	5	5½ fruit, 1 fat
1	0	10	1	17	1	1 fruit
2	0	280	5	29	2	2 starch
10	3	490	4	16	1	1 starch, 2 fat
24	5	530	14	29	2	2 starch, 1½ med. fat meat, 3 fat
3	1	470	9	4	0	1 veg, 1 lean meat
11	4	1410	10	19	1	1 starch, 1 med. fat meat, 1 fat
43	12	1420	20	16	1	3 veg or 1 starch, 2½ med. fat meat, 6 fat
13	7	780	19	14	1	3 veg or 1 starch, 2½ med. fat meat
47	13	1860	45	16	1	3 veg or 1 starch, 6 med. fat meat, 3 fat
27	7	190	6	47	3	3 other carb, 5 fat
17	6	240	4	48	3	3 other carb, 3 fat

1 Carbohydrate Choice = 1 starch or 1 fruit or 1 milk exchange
* Grams of fiber subtracted from total carbohydrate

MENU ITEM	SERVING SIZE	CALORIES	CALORIES FROM FAT
Oatmeal Raisin Cookie	1	320	110

SMART MEAL, BOSTON MARKET

¼ Chicken, White Meat (no skin or wing) New Potatoes Zucchini Marinara Honey Wheat Roll Margarine (1 pat)	**Calories:** **Fat:** **Carb Choices:** **Exchanges:**	565 18 grams 4½ 3½ starch, 2 veg, 4 very lean meat, 2 fat

Ham & Turkey Club Sandwich (no cheese or sauce) Fruit Salad	**Calories:** **Fat:** **Carb Choices:** **Exchanges:**	500 7 grams 5½ 4 starch, 1 fruit, 3 lean meat

BURGER KING
SANDWICHES

BK Big Fish™ Sandwich	1 (8.9 oz)	700	370
BK Broiler® Chicken Sandwich	1 (8.7 oz)	550	260
Cheeseburger	1 (4.8 oz)	380	170
Chicken Sandwich	1 (8 oz)	710	390
Double Cheeseburger	1 (7.4 oz)	600	320
Double Cheeseburger with Bacon	1 (7.6 oz)	640	350
Double Whopper® Sandwich	1 (12.3 oz)	870	500
Double Whopper® with Cheese Sandwich	1 (13.1 oz)	960	570

☀ Smart Choice

TOTAL FAT (g)	SATURATED FAT (g)	SODIUM (mg)	PROTEIN (g)	CARBOHYDRATE (g)	CARBOHYDRATE CHOICES	EXCHANGES
13	3	260	4	48	3	3 other carb, 2½ fat

SMART MEAL, BOSTON MARKET

Skinless Rotisserie Turkey Breast	**Calories:** 475
Homestyle Mashed Potatoes & Gravy	**Fat:** 12 grams
Steamed Vegetables	**Carb Choices:** 3½
Fruit Salad	**Exchanges:** 2 starch, 1 fruit, 1 veg, 5 very lean meat, 1½ fat

TOTAL FAT (g)	SATURATED FAT (g)	SODIUM (mg)	PROTEIN (g)	CARBOHYDRATE (g)	CARBOHYDRATE CHOICES	EXCHANGES
41	6	980	26	56	4	4 starch, 2½ med. fat meat, 5 fat
29	6	480	30	41	3	3 starch, 3½ med. fat meat, 2 fat
19	9	770	23	28	2	2 starch, 2½ med. fat meat, 1 fat
43	9	1400	26	54	3½	3½ starch, 3 med. fat meat, 5 fat
36	17	1060	41	28	2	2 starch, 5 med. fat meat, 2 fat
39	18	1240	44	28	2	2 starch, 5½ med. fat meat, 2 fat
56	19	940	46	45	3	3 starch, 5½ med. fat meat, 4 fat
63	24	1420	52	46	3	3 starch, 6½ med. fat meat, 5½ fat

1 Carbohydrate Choice = 1 starch or 1 fruit or 1 milk exchange
* Grams of fiber subtracted from total carbohydrate

MENU ITEM	SERVING SIZE	CALORIES	CALORIES FROM FAT
Hamburger	1 (4.4 oz)	330	140
Whopper Jr.® Sandwich	1 (5.7 oz)	420	220
Whopper Jr.® with Cheese Sandwich	1 (6.2 oz)	460	250
Whopper® Sandwich	1 (9.5 oz)	640	350
Whopper® with Cheese Sandwich	1 (10.1 oz)	730	410
OTHER ENTREES			
☀ Chicken Tenders®	8 (4.1 oz)	310	150
SIDE ORDERS			
Coated French Fries, medium (salted)	1 order (3.6 oz)	340	150
French Fries, medium (salted)	1 order (4.1 oz)	370	180
Onion Rings	1 order (4.3 oz)	310	130
SALADS			
☀ Broiled Chicken Salad	1 (10.6 oz)	200	90
☀ Garden Salad	1 (7.5 oz)	100	45
☀ Side Salad	1 (4.7 oz)	60	25
SALAD DRESSINGS			
Bleu Cheese Salad Dressing	1.1 oz	160	140
French Salad Dressing	1.1 oz	140	90
Ranch Salad Dressing	1.1 oz	180	170
☀ Italian Salad Dressing, Reduced Calorie Light	1.1 oz	15	5
Thousand Island Salad Dressing	1.1 oz	140	110
CONDIMENTS			
☀ Bacon Bits	0.1 oz	15	10

 Smart Choice

TOTAL FAT (g)	SATURATED FAT (g)	SODIUM (mg)	PROTEIN (g)	CARBOHYDRATE (g)	CARBOHYDRATE CHOICES	EXCHANGES
15	6	530	20	28	2	2 starch, 2 med. fat meat, 1 fat
24	8	530	21	29	2	2 starch, 2½ med. fat meat, 2 fat
28	10	770	23	29	2	2 starch, 2½ med. fat meat, 2½ fat
39	11	870	27	45	3	3 starch, 3 med. fat meat, 4 fat
46	16	1350	33	46	3	3 starch, 4 med. fat meat, 4 fat
17	4	710	21	19	1	1 starch, 3 med. fat meat
17	5	680	0	43	3	3 starch, 2½ fat
20	5	240	5	43	3	3 starch, 3 fat
14	2	810	4	35*	2	2½ starch, 2½ fat
10	4	110	21	7	½	½ starch or 2 veg, 3 lean meat
5	3	110	6	7	½	½ starch or 2 veg, 1 med. fat meat
3	2	55	3	4	0	1 veg, 1 fat
16	4	260	2	1	0	3 fat
10	2	190	0	11	1	1 other carb, 2 fat
19	4	170	<1	2	0	4 fat
1	0	50	0	3	0	free
12	3	190	0	7	½	½ other carb, 2 fat
1	<1	0	1	0	0	free

1 Carbohydrate Choice = 1 starch or 1 fruit or 1 milk exchange
* Grams of fiber subtracted from total carbohydrate

MENU ITEM	SERVING SIZE	CALORIES	CALORIES FROM FAT
☀ Barbecue Dipping Sauce	1 oz	35	0
☀ Bull's Eye® Barbecue Sauce	0.5 oz	20	0
☀ Croutons	0.2 oz	30	10
☀ Dip, A.M. Express®	1 oz	80	0
☀ Grape Jam, A.M. Express®	0.4 oz	30	0
☀ Honey Dipping Sauce	1 oz	90	0
☀ Ketchup	0.5 oz	15	0
Land O'Lakes® Whipped Classic Blend	0.4 oz	65	65
☀ Lettuce	0.7 oz	0	0
Mayonnaise	1 oz	210	210
☀ Mustard	0.1 oz	0	0
☀ Onion	0.5 oz	5	0
☀ Pickles	0.5 oz	0	0
Processed American Cheese	0.9 oz	90	70
Ranch Dipping Sauce	1 oz	170	160
☀ Strawberry Jam, A.M. Express®	0.4 oz	30	0
☀ Sweet & Sour Dipping Sauce	1 oz	45	0
Tartar Sauce	1 oz	180	175
☀ Tomato	1 oz	5	0

DESSERTS

Dutch Apple Pie	1 (4 oz)	300	140

SHAKES

Chocolate Shake, medium	10 oz	320	60
Strawberry Shake, medium	12 oz	420	50

☀ Smart Choice

TOTAL FAT (g)	SATURATED FAT (g)	SODIUM (mg)	PROTEIN (g)	CARBOHYDRATE (g)	CARBOHYDRATE CHOICES	EXCHANGES
0	0	400	0	9	½	½ other carb
0	0	140	0	5	0	free
1	0	75	<1	4	0	free
0	0	20	0	21	1½	1½ other carb
0	0	0	0	7	½	½ other carb
0	0	10	0	23	1½	1½ other carb
0	0	180	0	4	0	free
7	1	75	0	0	0	1 fat
0	0	0	0	0	0	free
23	3	160	0	<1	0	5 fat
0	0	40	0	0	0	free
0	0	0	0	1	0	free
0	0	140	0	0	0	free
8	5	420	6	0	0	1 high fat meat
17	3	200	0	2	0	3 fat
0	0	5	0	8	½	½ other carb
0	0	50	0	11	1	1 other carb
19	3	220	0	0	0	4 fat
0	0	0	0	1	0	free
15	3	230	3	39	2½	2½ other carb, 3 fat
7	4	230	9	54	3½	3½ other carb, 1 fat
6	4	260	9	83	5½	5½ other carb, 1 fat

1 Carbohydrate Choice = 1 starch or 1 fruit or 1 milk exchange
* Grams of fiber subtracted from total carbohydrate

MENU ITEM	SERVING SIZE	CALORIES	CALORIES FROM FAT
Vanilla Shake, medium	10 oz	300	50
SOFT DRINKS			
Coca-Cola Classic®, medium	22 oz	280	0
Diet Coke®, medium	22 oz	1	0
Sprite®, medium	22 oz	260	0
OTHER BEVERAGES			
Coffee, black	12.4 oz	5	0
☀ Milk, 2%	8.5 oz	130	45
☀ Orange Juice, Tropicana®	10.9 oz	140	0
BREAKFAST			
Biscuit with Bacon, Egg and Cheese	6 oz	510	280
Biscuit with Sausage	5.3 oz	590	360
Croissan'wich® with Sausage, Egg & Cheese	6.2 oz	600	410
French Toast Sticks	4.9 oz	500	240
Hash Browns	2.5 oz	220	110

SMART MEAL, BURGER KING

Hamburger with lettuce,
  tomato, pickles, ketchup
Side Salad
Italian Salad Dressing,
  Reduced Calorie Light (1.1 oz)
Diet Soft Drink

Calories: 425
Fat: 19 grams
Carb Choices: 2½
Exchanges: 2 starch, 1 veg,
2 med. fat meat,
2 fat

☀ Smart Choice

TOTAL FAT (g)	SATURATED FAT (g)	SODIUM (mg)	PROTEIN (g)	CARBOHYDRATE (g)	CARBOHYDRATE CHOICES	EXCHANGES
6	4	230	9	53	3½	3½ other carb, 1 fat
0	0	NA	0	70	4½	4½ other carb
0	0	NA	0	<1	0	free
0	0	NA	0	66	4½	4½ other carb
0	0	5	0	1	0	free
5	3	120	8	12	1	1 2% milk
0	0	0	2	33	2	2 fruit
31	10	1530	19	39	2½	2½ starch, 2 med. fat meat, 4 fat
40	13	1390	16	41	3	3 starch, 1½ med. fat meat, 6 fat
46	16	1140	22	25	1½	1½ starch, 3 med. fat meat, 6 fat
27	7	490	4	60	4	4 starch, 4 fat
12	3	320	2	25	1½	1½ starch, 2 fat

1 Carbohydrate Choice = 1 starch or 1 fruit or 1 milk exchange
* Grams of fiber subtracted from total carbohydrate

MENU ITEM	SERVING SIZE	CALORIES	CALORIES FROM FAT

CARL'S JR.
SANDWICHES

☀ BBQ Chicken Sandwich	1 (6.75 oz)	310	50
☀ Big Burger	1 (6.75 oz)	470	180
Carl's Catch Fish Sandwich™	1 (7.5 oz)	560	270
Chicken Club Sandwich	1 (8.75 oz)	550	260
Double Western Bacon Cheeseburger®	1 (11.5 oz)	970	510
Famous Big Star™ Hamburger	1 (8.5 oz)	610	340
Hamburger	1 (3 oz)	200	70
Hot & Crispy Sandwich	1 (5 oz)	400	200
Santa Fe Chicken Sandwich	1 (8 oz)	530	260
Super Star® Hamburger	1 (11.25 oz)	820	480
Western Bacon Cheeseburger®	1 (8 oz)	870	315

GREAT STUFF™ POTATOES

Bacon & Cheese Stuffed Potato	1 (14.5 oz)	630	260
Broccoli & Cheese Stuffed Potato	1 (14.5 oz)	530	190
☀ Plain Potato	1 (9.5 oz)	290	0
Sour Cream & Chive Stuffed Potato	1 (11 oz)	430	130

SIDE ORDERS

Chicken Stars, 6-piece	1 order (3 oz)	230	130
CrissCut Fries®, large	1 order (5.75 oz)	550	310
French Fries, regular	1 order (4.5 oz)	370	180
Hash Brown Nuggets	1 order (3.25 oz)	270	150
Onion Rings	1 order (5.25 oz)	520	230

☀ Smart Choice

TOTAL FAT (g)	SATURATED FAT (g)	SODIUM (mg)	PROTEIN (g)	CARBOHYDRATE (g)	CARBOHYDRATE CHOICES	EXCHANGES
6	2	830	31	34	2	2 starch, 4 very lean meat
20	8	810	25	46	3	3 starch, 3 med. fat meat
30	7	1220	17	49*	3	3 starch, 2 med. fat meat, 4 fat
29	8	1160	35	37	2½	2½ starch, 4 med. fat meat, 2 fat
57	27	1810	56	58	4	4 starch, 7 med. fat meat, 4 fat
38	11	890	26	42	3	3 starch, 3 med. fat meat, 4 fat
8	4	500	11	23	1½	1½ starch, 1 high fat meat
22	5	980	14	35	2	2 starch, 2 med. fat meat, 2 fat
30	7	1230	30	36	2½	2½ starch, 3½ med. fat meat, 2 fat
53	20	1030	43	41	3	3 starch, 5 med. fat meat, 5 fat
35	16	1490	34	59	4	4 starch, 4 med. fat meat, 3 fat
29	7	1720	20	70*	4½	4½ starch, 2 med. fat meat, 3 fat
22	5	930	11	68*	4½	4½ starch, 4 fat
0	0	40	6	62*	4	4 starch
14	3	160	8	64*	4	4 starch, 3 fat
14	3	450	13	11	1	1 starch, 1½ med. fat meat, 1 fat
34	9	1280	7	55	3½	3½ starch, 6 fat
20	7	240	4	44	3	3 starch, 3 fat
17	4	410	3	27	2	2 starch, 3 fat
26	6	840	8	63	4	4 starch, 5 fat

1 Carbohydrate Choice = 1 starch or 1 fruit or 1 milk exchange
* Grams of fiber subtracted from total carbohydrate

MENU ITEM	SERVING SIZE	CALORIES	CALORIES FROM FAT
Zucchini	1 order (6 oz)	380	210
SALADS			
☀ Charbroiled Chicken Salad-To-Go™	1 (12 oz)	260	80
☀ Garden Salad-To-Go™	1 (4.75 oz)	50	25
SALAD DRESSINGS			
Blue Cheese Salad Dressing	2 oz	310	310
☀ French Salad Dressing, Fat Free	2 oz	70	0
House Salad Dressing	2 oz	220	200
☀ Italian Salad Dressing, Fat Free	2 oz	15	0
Thousand Island Salad Dressing	2 oz	250	220
CONDIMENTS			
American Cheese	1 slice (0.5 oz)	60	45
☀ BBQ Sauce	1 oz	50	0
☀ Breadsticks	0.25 oz	35	5
☀ Croutons	0.25 oz	35	10
☀ Grape Jelly	0.5 oz	35	0
☀ Honey Sauce	1 oz	90	0
☀ Mustard Sauce	1 oz	45	5
☀ Salsa	1 oz	10	0
☀ Strawberry Jam	0.5 oz	35	0
☀ Sweet N'Sour Sauce	1 oz	50	0
Swiss Cheese	1 slice (0.5 oz)	45	30
☀ Table Syrup	1 oz	90	0

☀ Smart Choice

TOTAL FAT (g)	SATURATED FAT (g)	SODIUM (mg)	PROTEIN (g)	CARBOHYDRATE (g)	CARBOHYDRATE CHOICES	EXCHANGES
23	6	1040	7	38	2½	2½ starch, 4 fat
9	5	530	28	11	1	2 veg or 1 starch, 3½ lean meat
3	2	75	3	4	0	1 veg
34	6	360	2	1	0	7 fat
0	0	760	0	18	1	1 other carb
22	4	440	1	3	0	4 fat
0	0	800	0	4	0	free
24	4	540	<1	7	½	½ other carb, 4 fat
5	3	270	3	0	0	1 fat
0	0	270	<1	11	1	1 other carb
<1	0	60	1	7	½	½ starch
1	0	65	<1	5	0	free
0	0	0	0	9	½	½ other carb
0	0	5	0	23	1½	1½ other carb
<1	0	150	0	10	½	½ other carb
0	0	160	0	2	0	free
0	0	0	0	9	½	½ other carb
0	0	60	0	11	1	1 other carb
4	3	220	3	0	0	1 fat
0	0	5	0	22	1½	1½ other carb

1 Carbohydrate Choice = 1 starch or 1 fruit or 1 milk exchange
* Grams of fiber subtracted from total carbohydrate

MENU ITEM	SERVING SIZE	CALORIES	CALORIES FROM FAT
DESSERTS			
Cheese Danish	1 (4 oz)	400	200
Cheesecake (Strawberry Swirl)	1 (3.5 oz)	300	160
Chocolate Cake	1 (3 oz)	300	90
Chocolate Chip Cookie	1 (2.5 oz)	370	170
SHAKES			
Chocolate Shake, small	13.5 oz	390	60
Strawberry Shake, small	13.5 oz	400	60
Vanilla Shake, small	13.5 oz	330	70
SOFT DRINKS			
Coca-Cola Classic®, regular	16 oz	190	0
Diet 7 Up®, regular	16 oz	0	0
Diet Coke®, regular	16 oz	0	0
Dr. Pepper®, regular	16 oz	200	0
Minute Maid® Orange Soda, regular	16 oz	230	0
Ramblin® Root Beer, regular	16 oz	230	0
Sprite®, regular	16 oz	190	0
OTHER BEVERAGES			
Coffee, black	12 oz	10	0
Hot Chocolate, regular	12 oz	110	10
Iced Tea, regular	14 oz	5	0
☀ Orange Juice	6 oz	90	0
☀ Milk, 1%	10 oz	150	30

☀ Smart Choice

TOTAL FAT (g)	SATURATED FAT (g)	SODIUM (mg)	PROTEIN (g)	CARBOHYDRATE (g)	CARBOHYDRATE CHOICES	EXCHANGES
22	5	390	5	49	3	3 other carb, 4 fat
17	9	220	6	31	2	2 other carb, 3 fat
10	3	260	3	49	3	3 other carb, 2 fat
19	8	350	3	49	3	3 other carb, 3 fat
7	5	280	9	74	5	5 other carb, 1 fat
7	5	240	9	77	5	5 other carb, 1 fat
8	5	250	11	54	3½	3½ other carb, 1 fat
0	0	50	0	51	3½	3½ other carb
0	0	90	0	1	0	free
0	0	40	0	0	0	free
0	0	30	0	52	3½	3½ other carb
0	0	30	0	59	4	4 other carb
0	0	75	0	61	4	4 other carb
0	0	90	0	48	3	3 other carb
0	0	25	1	1	0	free
1	0	125	1	24	1½	1½ other carb
0	0	55	0	0	0	free
0	0	0	1	20	1	1 fruit
3	2	180	14	18	1	1 1% milk

1 Carbohydrate Choice = 1 starch or 1 fruit or 1 milk exchange
* Grams of fiber subtracted from total carbohydrate

MENU ITEM	SERVING SIZE	CALORIES	CALORIES FROM FAT
BREAKFAST			
Bacon	2 pieces	40	35
Blueberry Muffin	1 (4.25 oz)	340	120
Bran Muffin	1 (4.75 oz)	370	120
Breakfast Burrito	1 (5.25 oz)	430	230
☀ Breakfast Quesadilla	1 (5 oz)	300	130
Cinnamon Roll	1 (4.25 oz)	420	120
English Muffin with Margarine	1 (2.5 oz)	230	90
French Toast Dips® (syrup not included)	1 order (3.75 oz)	410	230
Sausage	1 patty	200	160
☀ Scrambled Eggs	1 order (3.5 oz)	160	100
Sunrise Sandwich®	1 (4.5 oz)	370	190

SMART MEAL, CARL'S JR.

BBQ Chicken Sandwich	**Calories:**	525
Garden Salad-To-Go™	**Fat:**	12 grams
Italian Salad Dressing, Fat Free (2 oz)	**Carb Choices:**	4
Milk, 1% (10 oz)	**Exchanges:**	2 starch, 1 1% milk, 1 veg, 4 very lean meat

☀ Smart Choice

TOTAL FAT (g)	SATURATED FAT (g)	SODIUM (mg)	PROTEIN (g)	CARBOHYDRATE (g)	CARBOHYDRATE CHOICES	EXCHANGES
4	2	125	3	0	0	1 fat
14	2	340	5	49	3	3 starch, 3½ fat
13	2	410	7	55*	3½	3½ starch, 2 fat
26	12	810	22	29	2	2 starch, 2½ med. fat meat, 2 fat
14	6	750	14	27	2	2 starch, 2 med. fat meat
13	4	570	9	68	4½	4½ other carb, 2 fat
10	2	330	5	30	2	2 starch, 2 fat
25	6	380	6	40	2½	2½ starch, 5 fat
18	7	530	7	0	0	1 high fat meat, 2 fat
11	4	125	13	1	0	2 med. fat meat
21	6	710	14	31	2	2 starch, 2 med. fat meat, 2 fat

SMART MEAL, CARL'S JR.

Breakfast Quesadilla
Orange Juice (6 oz)

Calories: 390
Fat: 14 grams
Carb Choices: 3
Exchanges: 2 starch, 1 fruit, 2 med. fat meat

1 Carbohydrate Choice = 1 starch or 1 fruit or 1 milk exchange
* Grams of fiber subtracted from total carbohydrate

MENU ITEM	SERVING SIZE	CALORIES	CALORIES FROM FAT
CHURCH'S CHICKEN			
CHICKEN PIECES			
☀ Breast	1 (2.8 oz)	200	112
☀ Leg	1 (2 oz)	140	82
Thigh	1 (2.8 oz)	230	146
☀ Wing	1 (3.1 oz)	250	145
CHICKEN TENDER STRIPS™			
☀ Chicken Tender Strips™, 4-piece	4.4 oz	320	144
☀ Chicken Tender Strips™, 5-piece	5.5 oz	400	180
Chicken Tender Strips™, 15-piece	16.5 oz	1,200	540
SIDE ORDERS			
☀ Cajun Rice	1 order (3.1 oz)	130	63
☀ Potatoes & Gravy	1 order (3.7 oz)	90	30

SMART MEAL, CHURCH'S CHICKEN

Chicken Tender Strips, 4-piece
Potatoes & Gravy
(Add fresh vegetables or fruit)

Calories: 410
Fat: 19 grams
Carb Choices: 2½
Exchanges: 2 starch, 3 med. fat meat

☀ Smart Choice

TOTAL FAT (g)	SATURATED FAT (g)	SODIUM (mg)	PROTEIN (g)	CARBOHYDRATE (g)	CARBOHYDRATE CHOICES	EXCHANGES
12	NA	510	19	4	0	3 med. fat meat
9	NA	160	12	2	0	2 med. fat meat
16	NA	520	16	5	0	2 med. fat meat, 1 fat
16	NA	540	19	8	½	½ starch, 2½ med. fat meat
16	NA	560	24	18	1	1 starch, 3 med. fat meat
20	NA	700	30	23	1½	1½ starch, 4 med. fat meat
60	NA	2100	90	68	4½	4½ starch, 12 med. fat meat
7	NA	260	1	16	1	1 starch, 1 fat
3	NA	520	1	14	1	1 starch

1 Carbohydrate Choice = 1 starch or 1 fruit or 1 milk exchange
* Grams of fiber subtracted from total carbohydrate

MENU ITEM	SERVING SIZE	CALORIES	CALORIES FROM FAT
DAIRY QUEEN/BRAZIER			
SANDWICHES			
☀ Chicken Breast Fillet Sandwich	1 (6.75 oz)	430	180
Chicken Breast Fillet Sandwich with Cheese	1 (7.25 oz)	480	230
DQ® Homestyle® Bacon Double Cheeseburger	1 (9 oz)	610	320
DQ® Homestyle® Cheeseburger	1 (5.4 oz)	340	150
☀ DQ® Homestyle® Hamburger	1 (4.9 oz)	290	110
☀ DQ® Homestyle® Deluxe Double Hamburger	1 (7.5 oz)	440	200
DQ® Homestyle® Deluxe Double Cheeseburger	1 (8.5 oz)	540	280
DQ® Homestyle® Double Cheeseburger	1 (7.75 oz)	540	280
DQ® Homestyle® Ultimate Burger	1 (9.5 oz)	670	390
Fish Fillet Sandwich	1 (6 oz)	370	150
Fish Fillet Sandwich with Cheese	1 (6.5 oz)	420	190
☀ Grilled Chicken Breast Fillet Sandwich	1 (6.5 oz)	310	90
HOT DOGS/CHILI DOGS			
Cheese Dog	1 (4 oz)	290	160
Chili Dog	1 (4.5 oz)	280	150
Chili 'n Cheese Dog	1 (5 oz)	330	190
Hot Dog	1 (3.5 oz)	240	120

☀ Smart Choice

TOTAL FAT (g)	SATURATED FAT (g)	SODIUM (mg)	PROTEIN (g)	CARBOHYDRATE (g)	CARBOHYDRATE CHOICES	EXCHANGES
20	4	760	24	37	2½	2½ starch, 3 med. fat meat
25	7	980	27	38	2½	2½ starch, 3 med. fat meat, 2 fat
36	18	1380	41	31	2	2 starch, 5 med. fat meat, 2 fat
17	8	850	20	29	2	2 starch, 2 med. fat meat, 1 fat
12	5	630	17	29	2	2 starch, 2 med. fat meat
22	10	680	30	29	2	2 starch, 4 med. fat meat
31	16	1130	36	31	2	2 starch, 4 med. fat meat, 2 fat
31	16	1130	35	30	2	2 starch, 4 med. fat meat, 2 fat
43	19	1210	40	29	2	2 starch, 5 med. fat meat, 3 fat
16	4	630	16	39	2½	2½ starch, 2 med. fat meat, 1 fat
21	6	850	19	40	2½	2½ starch, 2 med. fat meat, 2 fat
10	3	1040	24	30	2	2 starch, 3 lean meat
18	8	950	12	20	1	1 starch, 1 med. fat meat, 3 fat
16	6	870	12	21	1½	1½ starch, 1 med. fat meat, 2 fat
21	9	1090	14	22	1½	1½ starch, 1 med. fat meat, 3 fat
14	5	730	9	19	1	1 starch, 1 med. fat meat, 2 fat

1 Carbohydrate Choice = 1 starch or 1 fruit or 1 milk exchange
* Grams of fiber subtracted from total carbohydrate

MENU ITEM	SERVING SIZE	CALORIES	CALORIES FROM FAT
CHICKEN STRIPS			
Chicken Strip Basket with BBQ Sauce	1 (10.25 oz)	810	330
Chicken Strip Basket with Gravy	1 (13 oz)	860	380
SIDE ORDERS			
French Fries, small	1 order (2.5 oz)	210	90
French Fries, regular	1 order (3.5 oz)	300	120
French Fries, large	1 order (4.5 oz)	390	160
Onion Rings	1 order (3 oz)	240	110
ICE CREAM			
☀ DQ® Chocolate Soft Serve	½ cup (3.3 oz)	150	45
☀ DQ® Vanilla Soft Serve	½ cup (3.3 oz)	140	40
NONFAT FROZEN YOGURT			
☀ Cup of Yogurt, regular	1 (7 oz)	230	5
Yogurt Cone, regular	1 (7.5 oz)	280	10
CONES			
☀ Chocolate Cone, small	1 (5 oz)	240	70
Chocolate Cone, regular	1 (7.5 oz)	360	100
Dipped Cone, small	1 (5.5 oz)	340	150
Dipped Cone, regular	1 (8.25 oz)	510	220
☀ Vanilla Cone, small	1 (5 oz)	230	60
Vanilla Cone, regular	1 (7.5 oz)	350	90
Vanilla Cone, large	1 (9 oz)	410	110

 Smart Choice

TOTAL FAT (g)	SATURATED FAT (g)	SODIUM (mg)	PROTEIN (g)	CARBOHYDRATE (g)	CARBOHYDRATE CHOICES	EXCHANGES
37	9	1590	33	83*	5½	5½ starch, 3 med. fat meat, 3 fat
42	11	1820	35	83*	6	6 starch, 3 med. fat meat, 4 fat
10	2	115	3	29	2	2 starch, 2 fat
14	3	160	4	40	2½	2½ starch, 2½ fat
18	4	200	5	46*	3	3 starch, 3 fat
12	3	135	4	29	2	2 starch, 2 fat
5	4	75	4	22	1½	1½ other carb, 1 fat
5	3	70	3	22	1½	1½ other carb, 1 fat
<1	0	160	8	49	3	3 other carb
1	<1	170	9	59	4	4 other carb
8	5	115	6	37	2½	2½ other carb, 1 fat
11	8	180	9	56	4	4 other carb, 2 fat
17	9	130	6	42	3	3 other carb, 3 fat
25	13	200	9	63	4	4 other carb, 5 fat
7	5	115	6	38	2½	2½ other carb, 1 fat
10	7	170	8	57	4	4 other carb, 2 fat
12	8	200	10	65	4	4 other carb, 2 fat

1 Carbohydrate Choice = 1 starch or 1 fruit or 1 milk exchange
* Grams of fiber subtracted from total carbohydrate

MENU ITEM	SERVING SIZE	CALORIES	CALORIES FROM FAT
SUNDAES			
Chocolate Sundae, small	1 (6 oz)	290	60
Chocolate Sundae, regular	1 (8.5 oz)	410	90
Yogurt Strawberry Sundae, regular	1 (8 oz)	300	5
MISTY®			
☀ Misty® Slush, small	16 oz	220	0
Misty® Slush, regular	20 oz	290	0
☀ Strawberry Misty® Cooler	12 oz	190	0
MALTS/SHAKES			
Chocolate Malt, small	15 oz	650	150
Chocolate Malt, regular	20 oz	880	200
Chocolate Shake, small	14 oz	560	140
Chocolate Shake, regular	19 oz	770	180
BLIZZARD®			
Butterfinger® Blizzard®, small	12 oz	520	160
Butterfinger® Blizzard®, regular	16 oz	750	240
Chocolate Chip Cookie Dough Blizzard®, small	12 oz	660	220
Chocolate Chip Cookie Dough Blizzard®, regular	16 oz	950	320
Chocolate Sandwich Cookie Blizzard®, small	12 oz	520	160
Chocolate Sandwich Cookie Blizzard®, regular	16 oz	640	210
Heath® Blizzard®, small	12 oz	560	190

☀ Smart Choice

TOTAL FAT (g)	SATURATED FAT (g)	SODIUM (mg)	PROTEIN (g)	CARBOHYDRATE (g)	CARBOHYDRATE CHOICES	EXCHANGES
7	5	150	6	51	3½	3½ other carb, 1 fat
10	6	210	8	73	4½	4½ other carb, 2 fat
<1	<1	180	9	66	4	4 other carb
0	0	20	0	56	3½	3½ other carb
0	0	30	0	74	5	5 other carb
0	0	25	0	49	3	3 other carb
16	10	370	15	111	7½	7½ other carb, 3 fat
22	14	500	19	153	10	10 other carb, 4 fat
15	10	310	13	94	6	6 other carb, 3 fat
20	13	420	17	130	8½	8½ other carb, 4 fat
18	11	250	11	80	5	5 other carb, 3 fat
26	16	360	16	115	7½	7½ other carb, 5 fat
24	13	440	12	99	6½	6½ other carb, 4 fat
36	19	660	17	143	9½	9½ other carb, 6 fat
18	9	380	10	79	5	5 other carb, 3 fat
23	11	500	12	97	6½	6½ other carb, 4 fat
21	14	380	10	82	5½	5½ other carb, 4 fat

1 Carbohydrate Choice = 1 starch or 1 fruit or 1 milk exchange
* Grams of fiber subtracted from total carbohydrate

MENU ITEM	SERVING SIZE	CALORIES	CALORIES FROM FAT
Heath® Blizzard®, regular	16 oz	820	300
Reeses® Peanut Butter Cup Blizzard®, small	12 oz	590	210
Reeses® Peanut Butter Cup Blizzard®, regular	16 oz	790	300
Strawberry Blizzard®, small	12 oz	400	100
Strawberry Blizzard®, regular	16 oz	570	140
BREEZE®			
Heath® Breeze®, small	12 oz	470	90
Heath® Breeze®, regular	16 oz	710	170
Strawberry Breeze®, small	12 oz	320	5
Strawberry Breeze®, regular	16 oz	460	10
DQ® TREATZZA PIZZA™			
☀ Heath®	⅛ pizza (2.4 oz)	180	60
☀ M&M®	⅛ pizza (2.4 oz)	190	70
Peanut Butter Fudge	⅛ pizza (2.5 oz)	220	90
☀ Strawberry-Banana	⅛ pizza (2.7 oz)	180	50
DQ® FROZEN CAKES			
Heart Cake (undecorated)	⅒ cake (4.8 oz)	270	80
Log Cake	⅛ cake (4.75 oz)	280	80
Round Cake (8", undecorated)	⅛ cake (6.25 oz)	340	100
Round Cake (10", undecorated)	1/12 cake (6.5 oz)	360	110
Sheet Cake	1/20 cake (6 oz)	350	110

☀ Smart Choice

TOTAL FAT (g)	SATURATED FAT (g)	SODIUM (mg)	PROTEIN (g)	CARBOHYDRATE (g)	CARBOHYDRATE CHOICES	EXCHANGES
33	20	580	14	119	8	8 other carb, 6 fat
24	13	320	14	81	5½	5½ other carb, 4 fat
33	17	430	19	105	7	7 other carb, 6 fat
11	7	190	9	66	4½	4½ other carb, 2 fat
16	11	260	12	95	6	6 other carb, 3 fat
10	6	380	11	85	5½	5½ other carb, 2 fat
18	11	580	15	123	8	8 other carb, 3 fat
<1	<1	190	10	68	4½	4½ other carb
1	1	270	13	99	6½	6½ other carb
7	4	160	3	28	2	2 other carb, 1 fat
7	4	160	3	29	2	2 other carb, 1 fat
10	5	200	4	28	2	2 other carb, 2 fat
6	3	140	3	29	2	2 other carb, 1 fat
9	6	190	5	41	3	3 other carb, 1 fat
9	6	220	5	43	3	3 other carb, 1½ fat
12	7	250	7	53	3½	3½ other carb, 2 fat
12	8	260	7	55	3½	3½ other carb, 2 fat
12	7	270	7	54	3½	3½ other carb, 2 fat

1 Carbohydrate Choice = 1 starch or 1 fruit or 1 milk exchange
* Grams of fiber subtracted from total carbohydrate

MENU ITEM	SERVING SIZE	CALORIES	CALORIES FROM FAT
OTHER FROZEN TREATS			
Banana Split	1 (13 oz)	510	100
Buster Bar®	1 (5.25 oz)	450	260
Chocolate Dilly® Bar	1 (3 oz)	210	120
Chocolate Mint Dilly® Bar	1 (2.75 oz)	190	100
☀ DQ® Fudge Bar	1 (2.3 oz)	50	0
☀ DQ® Lemon Freez'r™	½ cup (3.25 oz)	80	0
☀ DQ® Sandwich (ice cream)	1 (2 oz)	150	45
☀ DQ® Vanilla Orange Bar	1 (2.3 oz)	60	0
Fudge Nut Bar™	1 (5 oz)	410	220
Peanut Buster® Parfait	1 (5.25 oz)	730	280
Queen's Choice® Chocolate Big Scoop®	1 (4 oz)	250	120
Queen's Choice® Vanilla Big Scoop®	1 (4 oz)	250	120
☀ Starkiss®	1 (3 oz)	80	0
Strawberry Shortcake	1 (8.5 oz)	430	120
Toffee Dilly® Bar with Heath® Pieces	1 (2.8 oz)	210	110

SMART MEAL, DAIRY QUEEN/BRAZIER

Grilled Chicken Breast Fillet Sandwich
(request lettuce and tomato)
Strawberry Misty® Cooler (12 oz)

Calories:	500
Fat:	10 grams
Carb Choices:	5½
Exchanges:	2 starch, 3 other carb, 3 lean meat

☀ Smart Choice

TOTAL FAT (g)	SATURATED FAT (g)	SODIUM (mg)	PROTEIN (g)	CARBOHYDRATE (g)	CARBOHYDRATE CHOICES	EXCHANGES
12	8	180	8	96	6½	6½ other carb, 2 fat
28	12	280	10	41	3	3 other carb, 5 fat
13	7	75	3	21	1½	1½ other carb, 2 fat
12	9	100	3	20	1	1 other carb, 2 fat
0	0	70	4	13	1	1 other carb
0	0	10	0	20	1	1 other carb
5	2	115	3	24	1½	1½ other carb, 1 fat
0	0	40	2	17	1	1 other carb
25	11	250	8	40	2½	2½ other carb, 5 fat
31	17	400	16	99	6½	6½ other carb, 6 fat
14	9	95	4	28	2	2 other carb, 2½ fat
14	9	100	4	27	2	2 other carb, 2½ fat
0	0	10	0	21	1½	1½ other carb
14	9	360	7	70	4½	4½ other carb, 3 fat
12	9	100	3	24	1½	1½ other carb, 2 fat

SMART MEAL, DAIRY QUEEN/BRAZIER

DQ® Homestyle® Hamburger
(request lettuce and tomato)
DQ® Sandwich (ice cream)

Calories: 440
Fat: 17 grams
Carb Choices: 3½
Exchanges: 2 starch,
1½ other
carb, 2 med.
fat meat, 1 fat

1 Carbohydrate Choice = 1 starch or 1 fruit or 1 milk exchange
* Grams of fiber subtracted from total carbohydrate

MENU ITEM	SERVING SIZE	CALORIES	CALORIES FROM FAT
DOMINO'S			
LARGE (14") CHEESE PIZZAS			
Deep Dish Pizza	2 slices (6.2 oz)	464	177
☀ Hand Tossed Pizza	2 slices (4.8 oz)	319	88
☀ Thin Crust Pizza	⅙ pizza (3.5 oz)	255	98
"ADD A TOPPING" FOR LARGE PIZZA, PER SLICE			
☀ Anchovies	NA	23	9
Bacon	NA	75	58
☀ Banana Peppers	NA	3	0
☀ Canned Mushrooms	NA	3	0
Cheddar Cheese	NA	48	35
Extra Cheese	NA	46	31
☀ Fresh Mushrooms	NA	3	0
☀ Green Olives	NA	11	11
☀ Green Peppers	NA	2	0
☀ Ham	NA	17	6
Italian Sausage	NA	44	31
☀ Onion	NA	3	0
Pepperoni	NA	55	45
☀ Pineapple Tidbits	NA	8	0
Pre-Cooked Beef	NA	44	36
☀ Ripe Olives	NA	12	10
MEDIUM (12") PIZZAS			
Deep Dish Pizza	2 slices (6.2 oz)	467	192

☀ Smart Choice

TOTAL FAT (g)	SATURATED FAT (g)	SODIUM (mg)	PROTEIN (g)	CARBOHYDRATE (g)	CARBOHYDRATE CHOICES	EXCHANGES
20	7	978	18	55	3½	3½ starch, 1½ med. fat meat, 2 fat
10	4	622	14	44	3	3 starch, 1 med. fat meat
11	4	710	11	28	2	2 starch, 1 med. fat meat, ½ fat
1	<1	395	3	0	0	free
6	2	207	4	0	0	1 fat
0	0	81	0	1	0	free
0	<1	50	0	1	0	free
4	2	73	3	0	0	1 fat
3	2	116	3	0	0	1 fat
0	<1	0	0	1	0	free
1	<1	227	0	0	0	free
0	0	0	0	1	0	free
1	<1	156	2	0	0	free
3	1	137	2	1	0	1 fat
0	0	0	0	1	0	free
5	2	177	2	0	0	1 fat
0	0	1	0	2	0	free
4	2	123	2	0	0	1 fat
1	<1	63	0	1	0	free
21	8	998	18	52	3½	3½ starch, 1½ med. fat meat, 2 fat

1 Carbohydrate Choice = 1 starch or 1 fruit or 1 milk exchange
* Grams of fiber subtracted from total carbohydrate

MENU ITEM	SERVING SIZE	CALORIES	CALORIES FROM FAT
Hand Tossed Pizza	2 slices (4.9 oz)	349	95
Thin Crust Pizza	¼ pizza (3.7 oz)	273	105
"ADD A TOPPING" FOR MEDIUM PIZZA, PER SLICE			
☀ Anchovies	NA	23	9
Bacon	NA	82	63
☀ Banana Peppers	NA	3	0
☀ Canned Mushrooms	NA	4	0
Cheddar Cheese	NA	57	42
Extra Cheese	NA	49	33
☀ Fresh Mushrooms	NA	4	0
☀ Green Olives	NA	12	12
☀ Green Peppers	NA	3	0
☀ Ham	NA	18	7
Italian Sausage	NA	55	39
☀ Onion	NA	4	0
Pepperoni	NA	62	51
☀ Pineapple Tidbits	NA	10	0
Pre-Cooked Beef	NA	55	44
☀ Ripe Olives	NA	14	11
6" DEEP DISH			
Cheese Pizza	1 pizza (7.5 oz)	591	245
"ADD A TOPPING" FOR 6" DEEP DISH, PER SLICE			
☀ Anchovies	NA	45	19
Bacon	NA	82	63

☀ Smart Choice

TOTAL FAT (g)	SATURATED FAT (g)	SODIUM (mg)	PROTEIN (g)	CARBOHYDRATE (g)	CARBOHYDRATE CHOICES	EXCHANGES
11	5	673	15	49	3	3 starch, 1 med. fat meat, 1 fat
12	5	759	12	30	2	2 starch, 1 med. fat meat, 1 fat
1	<1	395	3	0	0	free
7	2	226	4	0	0	1½ fat
0	0	92	0	1	0	free
0	<1	73	0	1	0	free
5	3	88	4	0	0	1 fat
4	2	125	3	0	0	1 fat
0	<1	1	0	1	0	free
1	<1	255	0	0	0	free
0	0	0	0	1	0	free
1	<1	162	2	0	0	free
4	2	171	2	2	0	1 fat
0	0	0	0	1	0	free
6	2	199	3	0	0	1 fat
0	0	1	0	2	0	free
5	2	154	3	0	0	1 fat
1	<1	71	0	1	0	free
27	10	1208	23	65	4	4 starch, 2 med. fat meat, 3 fat
2	<1	730	6	0	0	free
7	2	226	4	0	0	1½ fat

1 Carbohydrate Choice = 1 starch or 1 fruit or 1 milk exchange
* Grams of fiber subtracted from total carbohydrate

MENU ITEM	SERVING SIZE	CALORIES	CALORIES FROM FAT
☀ Banana Peppers	NA	3	0
☀ Canned Mushrooms	NA	2	0
Cheddar Cheese	NA	86	63
Extra Cheese	NA	59	40
☀ Fresh Mushrooms	NA	2	0
☀ Green Olives	NA	10	10
☀ Green Peppers	NA	2	0
☀ Ham	NA	17	6
Italian Sausage	NA	44	31
☀ Onion	NA	3	0
Pepperoni	NA	50	40
☀ Pineapple Tidbits	NA	5	0
Pre-Cooked Beef	NA	44	36
☀ Ripe Olives	NA	11	9
SIDE ORDERS			
☀ Barbecue Wings	1 piece (1 oz)	50	22
☀ Breadsticks	1 piece	78	30
☀ Cheesy Bread	1 piece	103	49
☀ Hot Wings	1 piece (1 oz)	45	22
SALADS			
☀ Garden Salad, small	1	22	2
☀ Garden Salad, large	1	39	4
MARZETTI® SALAD DRESSINGS			
Blue Cheese Salad Dressing	1.5 oz	220	216

☀ Smart Choice

TOTAL FAT (g)	SATURATED FAT (g)	SODIUM (mg)	PROTEIN (g)	CARBOHYDRATE (g)	CARBOHYDRATE CHOICES	EXCHANGES
0	0	73	0	0	0	free
0	0	36	0	0	0	free
7	4	132	5	0	0	1 fat
4	3	150	4	0	0	1 fat
0	0	0	0	0	0	free
1	<1	204	0	0	0	free
0	0	0	0	0	0	free
1	<1	156	2	0	0	free
3	1	137	2	1	0	1 fat
0	0	0	0	1	0	free
5	2	159	2	0	0	1 fat
0	0	0	0	1	0	free
4	2	123	2	0	0	1 fat
1	<1	57	0	0	0	free
2	<1	175	6	2	0	1 lean meat
3	<1	158	2	11	1	1 starch
5	2	182	3	11	1	1 starch, 1 fat
2	<1	354	5	1	0	1 lean meat
0	<1	14	1	4	0	1 veg
0	<1	26	2	8	½	1 veg
24	4	440	2	2	0	5 fat

1 Carbohydrate Choice = 1 starch or 1 fruit or 1 milk exchange
* Grams of fiber subtracted from total carbohydrate

MENU ITEM	SERVING SIZE	CALORIES	CALORIES FROM FAT
Creamy Caesar Salad Dressing	1.5 oz	200	198
Honey French Salad Dressing	1.5 oz	210	162
House Italian Salad Dressing	1.5 oz	220	216
☀ Italian Salad Dressing, Light	1.5 oz	20	9
Ranch Salad Dressing	1.5 oz	266	261
☀ Ranch Salad Dressing, Fat-Free	1.5 oz	40	0
Thousand Island Salad Dressing	1.5 oz	200	180

SMART MEAL, DOMINO'S

2 slices of Large Hand Tossed
   Cheese Pizza with fresh mushrooms,
   ham, and onion
Garden Salad, large
Italian Salad Dressing, Light (1.5 oz)

Calories: 424
Fat: 13 grams
Carb Choices: 4
Exchanges: 3 starch, 1 veg,
1 med. fat meat

HARDEE'S
SANDWICHES

	SERVING SIZE	CALORIES	CALORIES FROM FAT
Big Roast Beef™ Sandwich	1 (6.5 oz)	460	210
Cheeseburger	1 (4.3 oz)	310	130
☀ Chicken Fillet Sandwich	1 (7.5 oz)	480	160
Cravin' Bacon™ Cheeseburger	1 (8 oz)	690	410
Fisherman's Fillet™	1 (8.3 oz)	560	240
Frisco™ Burger	1 (8 oz)	720	410
☀ Grilled Chicken Sandwich	1 (7 oz)	350	100
☀ Hamburger	1 (4 oz)	270	100

☀ Smart Choice

TOTAL FAT (g)	SATURATED FAT (g)	SODIUM (mg)	PROTEIN (g)	CARBOHYDRATE (g)	CARBOHYDRATE CHOICES	EXCHANGES
22	3	470	1	2	0	4 fat
18	3	300	0	14	1	1 other carb, 3 fat
24	3	440	0	1	0	5 fat
1	0	780	0	2	0	free
29	4	380	0	1	0	6 fat
0	0	560	0	10	½	½ other carb
20	3	320	0	5	0	4 fat
24	9	1230	26	35	2	2 starch, 3 med. fat meat, 2 fat
14	6	890	16	30	2	2 starch, 2 med. fat meat, 1 fat
18	3	1280	26	54	3½	3½ starch, 3 med. fat meat
46	15	1150	30	38	2½	2½ starch, 4 med. fat meat, 4 fat
27	7	1330	26	54	3½	3½ starch, 3 med. fat meat, 2 fat
46	16	1340	33	43	3	3 starch, 4 med. fat meat, 4 fat
11	2	950	25	38	2½	2½ starch, 3 lean meat
11	3	670	14	29	2	2 starch, 2 med. fat meat

1 Carbohydrate Choice = 1 starch or 1 fruit or 1 milk exchange
* Grams of fiber subtracted from total carbohydrate

MENU ITEM	SERVING SIZE	CALORIES	CALORIES FROM FAT
☀ Hot Ham 'N' Cheese™	1 (5 oz)	310	100
Mesquite Bacon Cheeseburger	1 (4.5 oz)	370	160
Mushroom 'N' Swiss™ Burger	1 (6.8 oz)	490	220
Quarter Pound Double Cheeseburger	1 (6 oz)	470	240
Regular Roast Beef	1 (4.3 oz)	320	140
The Boss™	1 (7 oz)	570	300
The Works Burger	1 (8 oz)	530	270
FRIED CHICKEN			
☀ Breast	1 (5 oz)	370	130
☀ Leg	1 (2.5 oz)	170	60
Thigh	1 (4 oz)	330	130
Wing	1 (2.3 oz)	200	70
SIDE ORDERS			
☀ Baked Beans, small	1 order (5 oz)	170	10
Cole Slaw	1 order (4 oz)	240	180
French Fries, small	1 order (3.4 oz)	240	90
French Fries, medium	1 order (5 oz)	350	130
French Fries, large	1 order (6.1 oz)	430	160
☀ Gravy	1 (1.5 oz)	20	0
☀ Mashed Potatoes	1 order (4 oz)	70	0
SALADS			
Garden Salad	1 (10 oz)	220	120
☀ Grilled Chicken Salad	1 (11.5 oz)	150	30
☀ Side Salad	1 (4.6 oz)	25	0

 Smart Choice

TOTAL FAT (g)	SATURATED FAT (g)	SODIUM (mg)	PROTEIN (g)	CARBOHYDRATE (g)	CARBOHYDRATE CHOICES	EXCHANGES
12	6	1410	16	34	2	2 starch, 2 med. fat meat
18	7	970	19	32	2	2 starch, 2 med. fat meat, 1½ fat
25	12	1100	28	39	2½	2½ starch, 3½ med. fat meat, 1 fat
27	11	1290	27	31	2	2 starch, 3½ med. fat meat, 1½ fat
16	6	820	17	26	2	2 starch, 2 med. fat meat, 1 fat
33	12	910	27	42	3	3 starch, 3 med. fat meat, 3 fat
30	12	1030	25	41	3	3 starch, 3 med. fat meat, 2 fat
15	4	1190	29	29	2	2 starch, 3 med. fat meat
7	2	570	13	15	1	1 starch, 1½ med. fat meat
15	4	100	19	30	2	2 starch, 2 med. fat meat, 1 fat
8	2	740	10	23	1½	1½ starch, 1 high fat meat
1	0	600	8	32	2	2 starch
20	3	340	2	13	1	3 veg or 1 starch, 4 fat
10	3	100	4	33	2	2 starch, 2 fat
15	4	150	5	49	3	3 starch, 3 fat
18	5	190	06	59	4	4 starch, 3½ fat
trace	trace	260	trace	3	0	free
trace	trace	330	2	14	1	1 starch
13	9	350	12	11	1	2 veg, 1 med. fat meat, 2 fat
3	1	610	20	11	1	2 veg, 3 very lean meat
trace	trace	45	1	4	0	1 veg

1 Carbohydrate Choice = 1 starch or 1 fruit or 1 milk exchange
* Grams of fiber subtracted from total carbohydrate

MENU ITEM	SERVING SIZE	CALORIES	CALORIES FROM FAT
SALAD DRESSINGS			
☀ French Salad Dressing, Fat Free	2 oz	70	0
Ranch Salad Dressing	2 oz	290	260
Thousand Island Salad Dressing	2 oz	250	210
DESSERTS			
Big Cookie™	1 (2 oz)	280	110
☀ Chocolate Cone	1 (4 oz)	180	20
☀ Cool Twist™ Cone (Vanilla/Chocolate)	1 (4 oz)	180	20
Hot Fudge Sundae	1 (5.5 oz)	290	50
Peach Cobbler	1 (6 oz)	310	60
☀ Strawberry Sundae	1 (5.8 oz)	210	20
☀ Vanilla Cone	1 (4 oz)	170	20
SHAKES			
Chocolate Shake	12.3 oz	370	50
Peach Shake	12 oz	390	40
Strawberry Shake	12.8 oz	420	40
Vanilla Shake	12.3 oz	350	50
BREAKFAST			
Apple Cinnamon 'N' Raisin™ Biscuit	1 (2 oz)	200	70
Bacon and Egg Biscuit	1 (5.5 oz)	570	300
Bacon, Egg and Cheese Biscuit	1 (6 oz)	610	330
Big Country® Breakfast with Bacon	1 (9.5 oz)	820	440
Big Country® Breakfast with Sausage	1 (11.5 oz)	1000	590
Biscuit 'N' Gravy™	1 (7.8 oz)	510	250

☀ Smart Choice

TOTAL FAT (g)	SATURATED FAT (g)	SODIUM (mg)	PROTEIN (g)	CARBOHYDRATE (g)	CARBOHYDRATE CHOICES	EXCHANGES
0	0	580	0	17	1	1 other carb
29	4	510	1	6	0	6 fat
23	3	540	1	9	½	½ other carb, 4½ fat
12	4	150	4	41	3	3 other carb, 2 fat
2	1	110	5	34	2	2 other carb
2	1	120	4	34	2	2 other carb
6	3	310	7	51	3½	3½ other carb, 1 fat
7	1	360	2	60	4	4 other carb, 1 fat
2	1	140	5	43	3	3 other carb
2	1	130	4	34	2	2 other carb
5	3	270	13	67	4½	4½ other carb, 1 fat
4	3	290	10	77	5	5 other carb, 1 fat
4	3	270	11	83	5½	5½ other carb, 1 fat
5	3	300	12	65	4	4 other carb, 1 fat
8	2	350	2	30	2	2 starch, 1 fat
33	11	1400	22	45	3	3 starch, 2 med. fat meat, 4 fat
37	13	1630	24	45	3	3 starch, 2½ med. fat meat, 4 fat
49	15	1870	33	62	4	4 starch, 3½ med. fat meat, 6 fat
66	38	2310	41	62	4	4 starch, 5 med. fat meat, 7 fat
28	9	1500	10	55	3½	3½ starch, 5½ fat

1 Carbohydrate Choice = 1 starch or 1 fruit or 1 milk exchange
* Grams of fiber subtracted from total carbohydrate

MENU ITEM	SERVING SIZE	CALORIES	CALORIES FROM FAT
Country Ham Biscuit	1 (3.8 oz)	430	200
Frisco Breakfast Sandwich with Ham	1 (7.5 oz)	500	220
Ham Biscuit	1 (4 oz)	400	180
Ham, Egg and Cheese Biscuit	1 (6.5 oz)	540	270
Jelly Biscuit	1 (3.5 oz)	440	190
☀ Orange Juice	1 (12 oz)	140	0
☀ Pancakes	3 (4.8 oz)	280	20
Regular Hash Rounds™	16 (2.8 oz)	230	130
Rise 'N' Shine® Biscuit	1 (3 oz)	390	190
Sausage and Egg Biscuit	1 (12 oz)	630	360
Sausage Biscuit	1 (4 oz)	510	280
Ultimate Omelet™ Biscuit	1 (5.8 oz)	570	270

SMART MEAL, HARDEE'S

Hamburger
Baked Beans
Side Salad
French Salad Dressing, Fat Free (2 oz)

Calories: 535
Fat: 12 grams
Carb Choices: 5½
Exchanges: 4 starch, 1 other carb, 1 veg, 2 med. fat meat

TOTAL FAT (g)	SATURATED FAT (g)	SODIUM (mg)	PROTEIN (g)	CARBOHYDRATE (g)	CARBOHYDRATE CHOICES	EXCHANGES
22	6	1930	15	45	3	3 starch, 1½ med. fat meat, 2 fat
25	9	1370	24	46	3	3 starch, 3 med. fat meat, 1 fat
20	6	1340	9	47	3	3 starch, 1 med. fat meat, 2 fat
30	11	1660	20	48	3	3 starch, 2 med. fat meat, 4 fat
21	6	1000	6	57	4	3 starch, 1 other carb, 4 fat
trace	trace	5	2	34	2	2 fruit
2	1	890	8	56	4	4 starch
14	3	560	3	24	1½	1½ starch, 3 fat
21	6	1000	6	44	3	3 starch, 4 fat
40	22	1480	23	45	3	3 starch, 2 med. fat meat, 6 fat
31	10	1360	14	44	3	3 starch, 1 med. fat meat, 3½ fat
33	12	1370	22	45	3	3 starch, 2 med. fat meat, 4 fat

SMART MEAL, HARDEE'S

Hot Ham 'N' Cheese™ Sandwich
Side Salad
French Salad Dressing, Fat Free (2 oz)
Cool Twist™ Cone

Calories: 585
Fat: 14 grams
Carb Choices: 6
Exchanges: 2 starch, 3 other carb, 1 veg, 2 med. fat meat

1 Carbohydrate Choice = 1 starch or 1 fruit or 1 milk exchange
* Grams of fiber subtracted from total carbohydrate

MENU ITEM	SERVING SIZE	CALORIES	CALORIES FROM FAT
JACK IN THE BOX			
SANDWICHES			
Bacon Ultimate Cheeseburger	1 (10.5 oz)	1150	800
Cheeseburger	1 (4 oz)	330	140
Chicken Caesar Sandwich	1 (8.4 oz)	520	230
☀ Chicken Fajita Pita	1 (6.5 oz)	280	80
Chicken Sandwich	1 (6 oz)	450	230
Chicken Supreme	1 (8.3 oz)	680	400
Double Cheeseburger	1 (5.4 oz)	450	220
Grilled Chicken Fillet	1 (8.1 oz)	520	230
☀ Hamburger	1 (3.6 oz)	280	100
Jumbo Jack®	1 (7.8 oz)	560	320
Jumbo Jack® with Cheese	1 (8.7 oz)	650	390
☀ Philly Cheesesteak	1 (7.6 oz)	520	230
Quarter Pound Burger	1 (6 oz)	510	240
Sourdough Jack®	1 (7.9 oz)	670	390
Spicy Crispy Chicken	1 (7.9 oz)	560	240
Ultimate Cheeseburger	1 (9.8 oz)	1030	710
CHICKEN/FISH			
Chicken & Fries	1 order (9.4 oz)	730	310
☀ Chicken Breast Pieces, 5-piece	1 order (5.3 oz)	360	150
☀ Chicken Teriyaki Bowl	1 (17.7 oz)	670	40
Fish & Chips	1 order (9 oz)	720	320

☀ Smart Choice

TOTAL FAT (g)	SATURATED FAT (g)	SODIUM (mg)	PROTEIN (g)	CARBOHYDRATE (g)	CARBOHYDRATE CHOICES	EXCHANGES
89	30	1770	57	31	2	2 starch, 7½ med. fat meat, 10 fat
15	6	760	15	32	2	2 starch, 2 med. fat meat, ½ fat
26	6	1050	27	44	3	3 starch, 3 med. fat meat, 2 fat
9	4	840	24	25	1½	1½ starch, 3 lean meat
26	5	1030	16	38	2½	2½ starch, 2 med. fat meat, 3 fat
45	11	1500	23	46	3	3 starch, 2½ med. fat meat, 6 fat
24	12	970	24	35	2	2 starch, 3 med. fat meat, 1½ fat
26	6	1240	27	42	3	3 starch, 3 med. fat meat, 2½ fat
12	4	560	13	32	2	2 starch, 1½ med. fat meat
36	12	680	28	31	2	2 starch, 3½ med. fat meat, 3 fat
43	16	1090	32	32	2	2 starch, 4 med. fat meat, 4 fat
25	9	1980	33	41	3	3 starch, 4 med. fat meat
27	10	1080	26	39	2½	2½ starch, 3 med. fat meat, 2 fat
43	16	1180	32	39	2½	2½ starch, 4 med. fat meat, 4 fat
27	5	1020	24	55	3½	3½ starch, 3 med. fat meat, 2½ fat
79	26	1200	50	30	2	2 starch, 6½ med. fat meat, 9 fat
34	7	1690	26	79	5	5 starch, 2 med. fat meat, 4 fat
17	3	970	27	24	1½	1½ starch, 3½ med. fat meat
4	1	1620	29	123*	8	8 starch, 2 very lean meat
35	8	1580	19	81	5½	5½ starch, 1 med. fat meat, 5 fat

1 Carbohydrate Choice = 1 starch or 1 fruit or 1 milk exchange
* Grams of fiber subtracted from total carbohydrate

MENU ITEM	SERVING SIZE	CALORIES	CALORIES FROM FAT
TACOS			
Monster Taco	1 (4 oz)	290	160
Taco	1 (2.8 oz)	190	100
SIDE ORDERS			
Bacon & Cheddar Potato Wedges	1 order (9.4 oz)	800	520
Chili Cheese Curly Fries	1 order (8.1 oz)	650	370
Egg Rolls, 3-piece	1 order (6 oz)	440	220
Egg Rolls, 5-piece	1 order (10 oz)	730	370
Onion Rings	1 order (4.2 oz)	460	230
French Fries, regular	1 order (4.1 oz)	360	150
French Fries, jumbo	1 order (5 oz)	430	180
French Fries, Super Scoop	1 order (7 oz)	610	250
Seasoned Curly Fries	1 order (4.5 oz)	420	220
Stuffed Jalapenos, 7-piece	1 order (5.3 oz)	470	250
Stuffed Jalapenos, 10-piece	1 order (7.6 oz)	680	360
SALADS			
☀ Garden Chicken Salad	1 (8.9 oz)	200	80
☀ Side Salad	1 (3 oz)	50	30
SALAD DRESSINGS			
Blue Cheese Salad Dressing	2 oz	210	160
Buttermilk House Salad Dressing	2 oz	290	270
☀ Italian Salad Dressing, Low Calorie	2 oz	25	15
Thousand Island Salad Dressing	2 oz	250	220

☀ Smart Choice

TOTAL FAT (g)	SATURATED FAT (g)	SODIUM (mg)	PROTEIN (g)	CARBOHYDRATE (g)	CARBOHYDRATE CHOICES	EXCHANGES
18	6	550	11	21	1½	1½ starch, 1½ med. fat meat, 1½ fat
11	4	410	7	15	1	1 starch, 1 med. fat meat, 1 fat
58	16	1470	20	49	3	3 starch, 2 med. fat meat, 9 fat
41	12	1640	12	47*	3	3 starch, 8 fat
24	6	1020	15	40	2½	2½ starch, 1½ med. fat meat, 3 fat
41	10	1700	25	67	4½	4½ starch, 2 med. fat meat, 5 fat
25	5	780	7	50	3	3 starch, 5 fat
17	4	740	4	48	3	3 starch, 3 fat
20	5	890	4	58	4	4 starch, 3 fat
28	6	1250	6	77*	5½	5½ starch, 4 fat
24	5	1030	6	46	3	3 starch, 4 fat
28	11	1560	14	41	3	3 starch, 1 med. fat meat, 4 fat
40	15	2220	20	59	4	4 starch, 2 med. fat meat, 5 fat
9	4	420	23	8	½	1 veg, 3 lean meat
3	2	75	2	3	0	1 veg
18	4	750	1	11	1	1 other carb, 3 fat
30	11	560	1	6	½	½ other carb, 6 fat
2	0	670	0	2	0	free
24	4	570	1	10	½	½ other carb, 5 fat

1 Carbohydrate Choice = 1 starch or 1 fruit or 1 milk exchange
* Grams of fiber subtracted from total carbohydrate

MENU ITEM	SERVING SIZE	CALORIES	CALORIES FROM FAT
CONDIMENTS			
American Cheese	1 slice (0.4 oz)	45	35
☀ Barbeque Dipping Sauce	1 oz	45	0
Buttermilk House Dipping Sauce	1 oz	130	110
Country Crock Spread	1 pat (0.2 oz)	25	25
☀ Croutons	0.4 oz	50	15
☀ Ketchup	0.3 oz	10	0
☀ Pancake Syrup	1 pkt (1.5 oz)	120	0
☀ Salsa	1 oz	10	0
Sour Cream	1 pkt (1 oz)	60	50
☀ Soy Sauce	0.3 oz	5	0
☀ Sweet & Sour Dipping Sauce	1 oz	40	0
Swiss-Style Cheese	1 slice (0.4 oz)	40	25
Tartar Dipping Sauce	1.5 oz	220	210
DESSERTS			
Carrot Cake	1 (3.5 oz)	370	140
Cheesecake	1 (3.5 oz)	310	160
Double Fudge Cake	1 (3 oz)	300	90
Hot Apple Turnover	1 (3.8 oz)	340	160
SHAKES			
Cappucino Classic Ice Cream Shake, regular	10.8 oz	630	260
Chocolate Classic Ice Cream Shake, regular	10.9 oz	630	240

 Smart Choice

TOTAL FAT (g)	SATURATED FAT (g)	SODIUM (mg)	PROTEIN (g)	CARBOHYDRATE (g)	CARBOHYDRATE CHOICES	EXCHANGES
4	3	200	2	0	0	1 fat
0	0	300	1	11	1	1 other carb
13	5	240	<1	3	0	3 fat
3	<1	40	0	0	0	½ fat
2	<1	105	1	8	½	½ starch
0	0	100	0	3	0	free
0	0	5	0	30	2	2 other carb
0	0	200	0	2	0	free
6	4	30	1	1	0	1 fat
0	0	480	<1	<1	0	free
0	0	160	<1	11	1	1 other carb
3	2	190	3	0	0	1 fat
23	4	240	1	2	0	5 fat
16	3	340	3	54	3½	3½ other carb, 2½ fat
18	9	210	8	29	2	2 other carb, 3 fat
10	3	320	3	50	3	3 other carb, 2 fat
18	4	510	4	41	3	3 other carb, 3 fat
29	17	320	11	80	5	5 other carb, 5 fat
27	16	330	11	85	5½	5½ other carb, 5 fat

1 Carbohydrate Choice = 1 starch or 1 fruit or 1 milk exchange
* Grams of fiber subtracted from total carbohydrate

MENU ITEM	SERVING SIZE	CALORIES	CALORIES FROM FAT
Oreo Cookie Classic Ice Cream Shake, regular	11.7 oz	740	320
Strawberry Classic Ice Cream Shake, regular	10.5 oz	640	250
Vanilla Classic Ice Cream Shake, regular	10.8 oz	610	280
SOFT DRINKS			
Barq's Root Beer®, regular	20 oz	180	0
Coca-Cola Classic®, regular	20 oz	170	0
Diet Coke®, regular	20 oz	0	0
Dr. Pepper®, regular	20 oz	190	0
Sprite®, regular	20 oz	160	0
OTHER BEVERAGES			
☀ Milk, 2%	8 oz	130	45
Minute Maid® Lemonade, regular	20 oz	190	0
☀ Orange Juice	10.5 oz	150	0
BREAKFAST			
☀ Breakfast Jack	1 (4.3 oz)	300	110
☀ Grape Jelly	0.5 oz	40	0
Hash Brown	1 (2 oz)	160	100
Pancakes with Bacon	1 (5.6 oz)	400	110
Sausage Croissant	1 (6.4 oz)	670	430
Sourdough Breakfast Sandwich	1 (5.2 oz)	380	190
Supreme Croissant	1 (6 oz)	570	320

☀ Smart Choice

TOTAL FAT (g)	SATURATED FAT (g)	SODIUM (mg)	PROTEIN (g)	CARBOHYDRATE (g)	CARBOHYDRATE CHOICES	EXCHANGES
36	19	490	13	91	6	6 other carb, 6 fat
28	15	300	10	85	5½	5½ other carb, 5 fat
31	18	320	12	73	5	5 other carb, 5 fat
0	0	40	0	50	3	3 other carb
0	0	8	0	46	3	3 other carb
0	0	15	0	0	0	free
0	0	25	0	49	3	3 other carb
0	0	40	0	41	3	3 other carb
5	3	85	9	14	1	1 2% milk
0	0	90	0	48	3	3 other carb
0	0	20	2	34	2	2 fruit
12	5	890	18	30	2	2 starch, 2 med. fat meat
0	0	5	0	9	½	½ other carb
11	11	310	1	14	1	1 starch, 2 fat
12	3	980	13	59	4	4 starch, 2 fat
48	19	940	21	39	2½	2½ starch, 2 med. fat meat, 7 fat
21	8	1120	21	31	2	2 starch, 2 med. fat meat, 2 fat
36	7	1240	21	39	2½	2½ starch, 2 med. fat meat, 5 fat

1 Carbohydrate Choice = 1 starch or 1 fruit or 1 milk exchange
* Grams of fiber subtracted from total carbohydrate

MENU ITEM	SERVING SIZE	CALORIES	CALORIES FROM FAT
Ultimate Breakfast Sandwich	1 (8.5 oz)	620	320

SMART MEAL, JACK IN THE BOX

Hamburger	**Calories:**	355
Side Salad	**Fat:**	17 grams
Italian Salad Dressing,	**Carb Choices:**	2½
Low Calorie (2 oz)	**Exchanges:**	2 starch, 1 veg,
Diet Soft Drink		1½ med. fat meat

KFC
TENDER ROAST™ CHICKEN

MENU ITEM	SERVING SIZE	CALORIES	CALORIES FROM FAT
☀ Breast (with skin)	1 (4.9 oz)	251	97
☀ Breast (without skin)	1 (4.2 oz)	169	39
☀ Drumstick (with skin)	1 (1.9 oz)	97	39
☀ Drumstick (without skin)	1 (1.2 oz)	67	22
☀ Thigh (with skin)	1 (3.2 oz)	207	126
☀ Thigh (without skin)	1 (2.1 oz)	106	50
☀ Wing (with skin)	1 (1.8 oz)	121	69

ORIGINAL RECIPE® CHICKEN

Breast	1 (5.4 oz)	400	220
☀ Drumstick	1 (2.2 oz)	140	80
Thigh	1 (3.2 oz)	250	160
Whole Wing	1 (1.6 oz)	140	90

☀ Smart Choice

TOTAL FAT (g)	SATURATED FAT (g)	SODIUM (mg)	PROTEIN (g)	CARBOHYDRATE (g)	CARBOHYDRATE CHOICES	EXCHANGES
36	15	1800	36	39	2½	2½ starch, 4½ med. fat meat, 2 fat
11	3	830	37	1	0	5 lean meat
4	1	797	32	1	0	4½ very lean meat
4	1	271	15	<1	0	2 lean meat
2	<1	259	11	<1	0	1½ very lean meat
12	4	504	18	<2	0	2½ med. fat meat
6	2	312	13	<1	0	2 lean meat
8	2	331	12	1	0	2 med. fat meat
24	6	1116	29	16	1	1 starch, 4 med. fat meat, 1 fat
9	2	422	13	4	0	2 med. fat meat
18	5	747	16	6	½	½ starch, 2 med. fat meat, 2 fat
10	3	414	9	5	0	1 med. fat meat, 1 fat

1 Carbohydrate Choice = 1 starch or 1 fruit or 1 milk exchange
* Grams of fiber subtracted from total carbohydrate

MENU ITEM	SERVING SIZE	CALORIES	CALORIES FROM FAT
EXTRA TASTY CRISPY™ CHICKEN			
Breast	1 (5.9 oz)	470	250
🔆 Drumstick	1 (2.4 oz)	190	100
Thigh	1 (4.2 oz)	370	220
Whole Wing	1 (1.9 oz)	200	100
HOT & SPICY CHICKEN			
Breast	1 (6.5 oz)	530	310
🔆 Drumstick	1 (2.3 oz)	190	100
Thigh	1 (3.8 oz)	370	240
Whole Wing	1 (1.9 oz)	210	130
OTHER ENTREES			
Chunky Chicken Pot Pie	1 (13 oz)	770	378
🔆 Crispy Strips	3 (3.25 oz)	261	142
Hot Wings™, 6-piece	1 order (4.8 oz)	471	297
Kentucky Nuggets®, 6-piece	1 order (3.4 oz)	284	162
Original Recipe® Chicken Sandwich	1 (7.3 oz)	497	201
🔆 Value BBQ Flavored Chicken Sandwich	1 (5.3 oz)	256	74
SIDE ORDERS			
🔆 BBQ Baked Beans	1 order (5.5 oz)	190	25
Cole Slaw	1 order (5 oz)	180	80
🔆 Corn on the Cob	1 order (5 oz)	190	25
🔆 Garden Rice	1 order (4.4 oz)	120	10
🔆 Green Beans	1 order (4.7 oz)	45	15

 Smart Choice

TOTAL FAT (g)	SATURATED FAT (g)	SODIUM (mg)	PROTEIN (g)	CARBOHYDRATE (g)	CARBOHYDRATE CHOICES	EXCHANGES
28	7	930	31	25	1½	1½ starch, 4 med. fat meat, 1½ fat
11	3	260	13	8	½	½ starch, 2 med. fat meat
25	6	540	19	18	1	1 starch, 2 med. fat meat, 3 fat
13	4	290	10	10	½	½ starch, 1 med. fat meat, 2 fat
35	8	1110	32	23	1½	1½ starch, 4 med. fat meat, 3 fat
11	3	300	13	10	½	½ starch, 2 med. fat meat
27	7	570	18	13	1	1 starch, 2 med. fat meat, 3 fat
15	4	340	10	9	½	½ starch, 1 med. fat meat, 2 fat
42	13	2160	29	64*	4	4 starch, 3 med. fat meat, 4 fat
16	4	658	20	10	½	½ starch, 3 med. fat meat
33	8	1230	27	18	1	1 starch, 3½ med. fat meat, 3 fat
18	4	865	16	15	1	1 starch, 2 med. fat meat, 1½ fat
22	5	1213	29	46	3	3 starch, 3 med. fat meat, 1fat
8	1	782	17	28	2	2 starch, 2 lean meat
3	1	760	6	27*	2	2 starch, ½ fat
9	2	280	2	21	1½	1½ starch, 2 fat
3	<1	20	5	34	2	2 starch, ½ fat
1	0	890	3	23	1½	1½ starch
2	<1	730	1	7	½	1 veg

1 Carbohydrate Choice = 1 starch or 1 fruit or 1 milk exchange
* Grams of fiber subtracted from total carbohydrate

MENU ITEM	SERVING SIZE	CALORIES	CALORIES FROM FAT
☀ Macaroni & Cheese	1 order (5.4 oz)	180	70
☀ Mashed Potatoes with Gravy	1 order (4.8 oz)	120	50
☀ Mean Greens™	1 order (5.4 oz)	70	30
Potato Salad	1 order (5.6 oz)	230	130
Potato Wedges	1 order (4.8 oz)	280	120
☀ Red Beans & Rice	1 order (4.5 oz)	130	30
BREADS			
Biscuit	1 (2 oz)	180	80
Cornbread	1 (2 oz)	228	117

SMART MEAL, KFC

Tender Roast™ Chicken Breast (without skin)	**Calories:**	594
BBQ Baked Beans	**Fat:**	12 grams
Green Beans	**Carb Choices:**	4½
	Exchanges:	4 starch, 1 veg, 4½ very lean meat, 1 fat

☀ Smart Choice

TOTAL FAT (g)	SATURATED FAT (g)	SODIUM (mg)	PROTEIN (g)	CARBOHYDRATE (g)	CARBOHYDRATE CHOICES	EXCHANGES
8	3	860	7	21	1½	1½ starch, 1 fat
6	1	440	1	17	1	1 starch, 1 fat
3	1	650	4	11	1	1 starch
14	2	540	4	23	1½	1½ starch, 3 fat
13	4	750	5	28	2	2 starch, 2½ fat
3	1	360	5	21	1½	1½ starch
10	3	560	4	20	1	1 starch, 2 fat
13	2	194	3	25	1½	1½ starch, 2½ fat

1 Carbohydrate Choice = 1 starch or 1 fruit or 1 milk exchange
* Grams of fiber subtracted from total carbohydrate

MENU ITEM	SERVING SIZE	CALORIES	CALORIES FROM FAT
LITTLE CAESAR'S			
PIZZA!PIZZA!®			
Cheese Pizza, medium	1 slice	201	63
Pepperoni Pizza, medium	1 slice	220	78
PAN!PAN!® PIZZA			
☼ Cheese Pizza, medium	1 slice	181	55
☼ Pepperoni Pizza, medium	1 slice	199	69
Baby Pan!Pan!® Pizza	1 pizza	616	218
HOT OVEN-BAKED SANDWICHES			
Cheeser Sandwich	1 (12.1 oz)	822	355
Meatsa Sandwich	1 (15 oz)	1036	499
Pepperoni Sandwich	1 (11.2 oz)	899	425
Supreme Sandwich	1 (13.1 oz)	894	412
Veggie Sandwich	1 (13.7 oz)	669	215
COLD DELI-STYLE SANDWICHES			
Ham & Cheese Sandwich	1 (11.6 oz)	728	318
Italian Sandwich	1 (11.9 oz)	740	335
Veggie Sandwich	1 (11.9 oz)	647	261
SIDE ORDERS			
☼ Crazy Bread®	1 piece (1.4 oz)	106	31
☼ Crazy Sauce	1 pkt (6 oz)	74	4
SALADS			
☼ Antipasto Salad	1 (8.4 oz)	176	106

☼ Smart Choice

TOTAL FAT (g)	SATURATED FAT (g)	SODIUM (mg)	PROTEIN (g)	CARBOHYDRATE (g)	CARBOHYDRATE CHOICES	EXCHANGES
7	4	281	11	24	1½	1½ starch, 1 high fat meat
9	4	358	12	24	1½	1½ starch, 1 med. fat meat, 1 fat
6	3	379	9	22	1½	1½ starch, 1 med. fat meat
8	4	452	11	22	1½	1½ starch, 1 med. fat meat
24	12	1466	33	67	4½	4½ starch, 3 med. fat meat, 1 fat
39	20	2244	40	70*	4½	4½ starch, 4 high fat meat, 4 fat
56	24	3302	55	70*	4½	4½ starch, 6 med. fat meat, 5 fat
47	23	2428	43	74*	5	5 starch, 4 med. fat meat, 4 fat
46	21	2367	41	72*	5	5 starch, 4 med. fat meat, 5 fat
24	14	1534	33	73*	5	5 starch, 3 med. fat meat, 1 fat
35	13	1602	30	71	4½	4½ starch, 3 med. fat meat, 4 fat
37	12	1831	29	71	4½	4½ starch, 3 med. fat meat, 4 fat
29	9	1195	22	74	5	5 starch, 2 med. fat meat, 3 fat
3	<1	114	3	16	1	1 starch, ½ fat
<1	0	381	5	14	1	1 other carb
12	2	542	12	7	½	2 veg, 1 med. fat meat, 1 fat

1 Carbohydrate Choice = 1 starch or 1 fruit or 1 milk exchange
* Grams of fiber subtracted from total carbohydrate

MENU ITEM	SERVING SIZE	CALORIES	CALORIES FROM FAT
☀ Caesar Salad	1 (5 oz)	140	49
☀ Greek Salad	1 (10.3 oz)	168	86
☀ Tossed Salad	1 (8.5 oz)	116	27
SALAD DRESSINGS			
Blue Cheese Salad Dressing	1 pkt (1.5 oz)	160	124
Caesar Salad Dressing	1 pkt (1.5 oz)	255	239
French Salad Dressing	1 pkt (1.5 oz)	166	141
Greek Salad Dressing	1 pkt (1.5 oz)	268	269
Italian Salad Dressing	1 pkt (1.5 oz)	200	187
☀ Italian Salad Dressing, Fat-Free	1 pkt (1.5 oz)	15	0
Ranch Salad Dressing	1 pkt (1.5 oz)	221	197
Thousand Island Salad Dressing	1 pkt (1.5 oz)	183	153

SMART MEAL, LITTLE CAESAR'S

Cheese Pan Pan® Pizza (2 slices)
Caesar Salad
Italian Salad Dressing, Fat Free (1.5 oz)

Calories: 517
Fat: 17 grams
Carb Choices: 4
Exchanges: 3 starch, 3 veg, 3 med. fat meat

☀ Smart Choice

TOTAL FAT (g)	SATURATED FAT (g)	SODIUM (mg)	PROTEIN (g)	CARBOHYDRATE (g)	CARBOHYDRATE CHOICES	EXCHANGES
5	3	372	9	14	1	3 veg or 1 starch, 1 med. fat meat
10	<1	653	9	12	1	2 veg, 1 med. fat meat, 1 fat
3	<1	170	5	19	1	3 veg or 1 starch, ½ fat
14	2	600	NA	8	½	½ other carb, 3 fat
27	4	404	NA	3	0	5 fat
16	2	553	NA	6	0	3 fat
30	8	202	NA	0	0	6 fat
21	3	468	NA	3	0	4 fat
0	0	420	NA	3	0	free
22	3	340	NA	5	0	4 fat
17	3	542	NA	6	0	3 fat

1 Carbohydrate Choice = 1 starch or 1 fruit or 1 milk exchange
* Grams of fiber subtracted from total carbohydrate

MENU ITEM	SERVING SIZE	CALORIES	CALORIES FROM FAT
MCDONALD'S			
SANDWICHES			
Arch Deluxe™	1 (8.4 oz)	550	280
Arch Deluxe™ with Bacon	1 (8.7 oz)	590	310
Big Mac®	1 (7.6 oz)	560	280
Cheeseburger	1 (4.2 oz)	320	120
Crispy Chicken Biscuit	1 (5.5 oz)	430	190
Crispy Chicken Deluxe™	1 (7.8 oz)	500	220
Fish Filet Deluxe™	1 (8 oz)	560	250
Grilled Chicken Deluxe™	1 (7.8 oz)	440	180
☀ Grilled Chicken Deluxe™ (plain)	1 (7.25 oz)	300	45
☀ Hamburger	1 (3.7 oz)	260	80
McRib™	1 (7 oz)	490	220
☀ Quarter Pounder®	1 (6 oz)	420	190
Quarter Pounder® with Cheese	1 (7 oz)	530	270
CHICKEN MCNUGGETS®			
Chicken McNuggets®, 4-Piece	1 order (2.5 oz)	190	100
Chicken McNuggets®, 6-Piece	1 order (3.7 oz)	290	150
Chicken McNuggets®, 9-Piece	1 order (5.6 oz)	430	230
SIDE ORDERS			
French Fries, small	1 order (2.4 oz)	210	90
French Fries, large	1 order (5.1 oz)	450	200
French Fries, Super Size®	1 order (6.2 oz)	540	230

☀ Smart Choice

TOTAL FAT (g)	SATURATED FAT (g)	SODIUM (mg)	PROTEIN (g)	CARBOHYDRATE (g)	CARBOHYDRATE CHOICES	EXCHANGES
31	11	1010	28	39	3	2½ starch, 3 med. fat meat, 3 fat
34	12	1150	32	39	3	2½ starch, 4 med. fat meat, 3 fat
31	10	1070	26	45	3	3 starch, 3 med. fat meat, 3 fat
13	6	820	15	35	2	2 starch, 1½ med. fat meat, 1 fat
21	5	1340	20	40	2½	2½ starch, 2 med. fat meat, 2 fat
25	4	1100	26	43	3	3 starch, 3 med. fat meat, 2 fat
28	6	1060	23	54	4	3½ starch, 2½ med. fat meat, 3 fat
20	3	1040	27	38	3	2½ starch, 3 med. fat meat, 1 fat
5	1	930	27	38	2½	2½ starch, 3 very lean meat
9	4	580	13	34	2	2 starch, 1½ med. fat meat
25	9	970	24	42	2	2 starch, 2½ med. fat meat, 2 fat
21	8	820	23	37	2½	2½ starch, 3 med. fat meat
30	13	1290	28	38	2½	2½ starch, 3½ med. fat meat, 2 fat
11	3	340	12	10	1	1 starch, 1 med. fat meat, 1 fat
17	4	510	18	15	1	1 starch, 2 med. fat meat, 1 fat
26	5	770	27	23	1½	1½ starch, 3 med. fat meat, 2 fat
10	2	135	3	26	1½	1½ starch, 2 fat
22	4	290	6	52*	3½	3½ starch, 4 fat
26	5	350	8	62*	4	4 starch, 5 fat

1 Carbohydrate Choice = 1 starch *or* 1 fruit *or* 1 milk exchange
* Grams of fiber subtracted from total carbohydrate

MENU ITEM	SERVING SIZE	CALORIES	CALORIES FROM FAT
SALADS			
☀ Garden Salad	1 (6.2 oz)	35	0
☀ Grilled Chicken Deluxe Salad	1 (7.5 oz)	120	10
SALAD DRESSINGS			
Caesar Salad Dressing	1 pkt (1.8 oz)	160	130
☀ Herb Vinaigrette Salad Dressing, Fat Free	1 pkt (1.8 oz)	50	0
Ranch Salad Dressing	1 pkt (1.8 oz)	230	180
☀ Red French Salad Dressing, Reduced Calorie	1 pkt (1.8 oz)	160	70
CONDIMENTS			
☀ Barbeque Sauce	1 pkt (1 oz)	45	0
☀ Croutons	1 pkt (0.4 oz)	50	10
☀ Honey	1 pkt (0.5 oz)	45	0
Honey Mustard	1 pkt (0.5 oz)	50	40
Hot Mustard	1 pkt (0.5 oz)	60	30
Light Mayonnaise	1 pkt (0.4 oz)	40	35
Margarine	2 pats (0.4 oz)	90	90
☀ Sweet 'N Sour Sauce	1 pkt (1 oz)	50	0
☀ Syrup	1 pkt (2.1 oz)	180	0
DESSERTS			
Baked Apple Pie	1 (2.7 oz)	260	120
Chocolate Chip Cookie	1 (1.2 oz)	170	90
☀ McDonaldland® Cookies	1 pkg (1.5 oz)	180	45

☀ Smart Choice

TOTAL FAT (g)	SATURATED FAT (g)	SODIUM (mg)	PROTEIN (g)	CARBOHYDRATE (g)	CARBOHYDRATE CHOICES	EXCHANGES
0	0	20	2	7	½	1 veg
2	0	240	21	7	½	1 veg, 3 very lean meat
14	3	450	2	7	½	½ other carb, 3 fat
0	0	330	0	11	½	½ other carb
21	3	550	1	10	½	½ other carb, 4 fat
8	1	490	0	23	1½	1½ other carb, 1 fat
0	0	250	0	10	1	1 other carb
2	0	80	2	7	½	½ starch
0	0	0	0	12	1	1 other carb
5	<1	85	0	3	0	1 fat
4	0	240	1	7	½	½ other carb, ½ fat
4	<1	85	0	<1	0	1 fat
9	2	130	0	0	0	2 fat
0	0	140	0	11	1	1 other carb
0	0	20	0	47	3	3 other carb
13	4	200	3	34	2	2½ other carb, 3 fat
10	6	120	2	22	1½	1½ other carb, 2 fat
5	1	190	3	32	2	2 other carb, 1 fat

1 Carbohydrate Choice = 1 starch or 1 fruit or 1 milk exchange
* Grams of fiber subtracted from total carbohydrate

MENU ITEM	SERVING SIZE	CALORIES	CALORIES FROM FAT
Nuts (for Sundaes)	1 (0.2 oz)	40	30
Hot Caramel Sundae	1 (6.4 oz)	360	90
Hot Fudge Sundae	1 (6.3 oz)	340	100
Strawberry Sundae	1 (6.2 oz)	290	70
☀ Vanilla Ice Cream Cone, Reduced Fat	1 (3.2 oz)	150	40

SHAKES

Chocolate Shake, small	12.4 oz	360	80
Strawberry Shake, small	12.4 oz	360	80
Vanilla Shake, small	12.4 oz	360	80

SOFT DRINKS

Coca-Cola Classic®, child	12 oz	110	0
Coca-Cola Classic®, small	16 oz	150	0
Coca-Cola Classic®, medium	21 oz	210	0
Coca-Cola Classic®, large	32 oz	310	0
Diet Coke®, child	12 oz	0	0
Diet Coke®, small	16 oz	0	0
Diet Coke®, medium	21 oz	0	0
Diet Coke®, large	32 oz	0	0
Hi-C® Orange Drink, child	12 oz	120	0
Hi-C® Orange Drink, small	16 oz	160	0
Hi-C® Orange Drink, medium	21 oz	240	0
Hi-C® Orange Drink, large	32 oz	350	0
Sprite®, child	12 oz	110	0
Sprite®, small	16 oz	150	0

 Smart Choice

TOTAL FAT (g)	SATURATED FAT (g)	SODIUM (mg)	PROTEIN (g)	CARBOHYDRATE (g)	CARBOHYDRATE CHOICES	EXCHANGES
4	0	0	2	2	0	1 fat
10	6	180	7	61	4	4 other carb, 2 fat
12	9	170	8	52	3½	3½ other carb, 2 fat
7	5	95	7	50	3½	3½ other carb, 1 fat
5	3	75	4	23	1½	1½ other carb, 1 fat
9	6	250	11	60	4	4 other carb, 2 fat
9	6	180	11	60	4	4 other carb, 2 fat
9	6	250	11	59	4	4 other carb, 2 fat
0	0	10	0	29	2	2 other carb
0	0	15	0	40	2½	2½ other carb
0	0	20	0	58	4	4 other carb
0	0	30	0	86	6	6 other carb
0	0	20	0	0	0	free
0	0	30	0	0	0	free
0	0	40	0	0	0	free
0	0	60	0	0	0	free
0	0	20	0	32	2	2 other carb
0	0	30	0	44	2½	3 other carb
0	0	40	0	64	4	4 other carb
0	0	60	0	94	6	6 other carb
0	0	40	0	28	2	2 other carb
0	0	55	0	39	2½	2½ other carb

1 Carbohydrate Choice = 1 starch or 1 fruit or 1 milk exchange
* Grams of fiber subtracted from total carbohydrate

MENU ITEM	SERVING SIZE	CALORIES	CALORIES FROM FAT
Sprite®, medium	21 oz	210	0
Sprite®, large	32 oz	310	0
OTHER BEVERAGES			
☀ Milk, 1%	8 oz	100	20
☀ Orange Juice	6 oz	80	0
BREAKFAST			
Apple Danish	1 (3.7 oz)	360	140
Bacon, Egg & Cheese Biscuit	1 (5 oz)	440	230
Biscuit	1 (2.7 oz)	260	120
Breakfast Burrito	1 (4.1 oz)	320	180
Cheese Danish	1 (3.7 oz)	410	200
Cinnamon Roll	1 (3.3 oz)	400	180
☀ Egg McMuffin®	1 (4.8 oz)	290	110
☀ English Muffin	1 (1.9 oz)	140	20
☀ Hash Browns	1 order (1.9 oz)	130	70
☀ Hotcakes (plain)	1 order (5.3 oz)	310	60
☀ Hotcakes (with syrup)	1 order (7.4 oz)	490	60
Hotcakes (with syrup and 2 pats margarine)	1 order (7.8 oz)	580	150
☀ Lowfat Apple Bran Muffin	1 (4 oz)	300	30
Sausage	1 order (1.5 oz)	170	150
Sausage Biscuit	1 (4.2 oz)	430	260
Sausage Biscuit with Egg	1 (6 oz)	510	310
Sausage McMuffin®	1 (3.9 oz)	360	210

☀ Smart Choice

TOTAL FAT (g)	SATURATED FAT (g)	SODIUM (mg)	PROTEIN (g)	CARBOHYDRATE (g)	CARBOHYDRATE CHOICES	EXCHANGES
0	0	80	0	56	4	4 other carb
0	0	115	0	83	6	6 other carb
3	2	115	8	13	1	1 1% milk
0	0	20	1	20	1	1 fruit
16	5	290	5	51	3	3 starch, 3 fat
26	8	1310	17	33	2	2 starch, 2 med. fat meat, 3 fat
13	3	840	4	32	2	2 starch, 2 fat
20	7	600	13	23	1½	1½ starch, 1½ med. fat meat, 2 fat
22	8	340	7	47	3	3 starch, 4 fat
20	5	340	7	47	3	3 starch, 4 fat
12	5	710	17	27	2	2 starch, 2 med. fat meat
2	0	210	4	25	2	2 starch
8	2	330	1	14	1	1 starch, 1 fat
7	2	610	9	53	3½	3½ starch, 1 fat
7	2	630	9	100	6	3 starch, 3 other carb, 1 fat
16	3	760	9	100	6.5	3½ starch, 3 other carb, 3 fat
3	<1	380	6	61	4	4 starch
16	5	290	6	0	0	1 high fat meat, 1½ fat
29	9	1130	10	32	2	2 starch, 1 med. fat meat, 4½ fat
35	10	1210	16	33	2	2 starch, 2 med. fat meat, 5 fat
23	8	740	13	26	2	2 starch, 1 med. fat meat, 3 fat

1 Carbohydrate Choice = 1 starch or 1 fruit or 1 milk exchange
* Grams of fiber subtracted from total carbohydrate

MENU ITEM	SERVING SIZE	CALORIES	CALORIES FROM FAT
Sausage McMuffin® with Egg	1 (5.7 oz)	440	250
☀ Scrambled Eggs (2)	1 order (3.6 oz)	160	100

SMART MEAL, MCDONALD'S

Grilled Chicken Deluxe™ (plain)
Garden Salad
Herb Vinaigrette Salad Dressing,
  Fat Free (1 pkt)
Diet Soft Drink

Calories: 385
Fat: 5 grams
Carb Choices: 3½
Exchanges: 2½ starch, ½ other carb, 1 veg, 3 very lean meat

Egg McMuffin®
Orange Juice (6 oz)

Calories: 370
Fat: 12 grams
Carb Choices: 3
Exchanges: 2 starch, 1 fruit, 2 med. fat meat

☀ Smart Choice

TOTAL FAT (g)	SATURATED FAT (g)	SODIUM (mg)	PROTEIN (g)	CARBOHYDRATE (g)	CARBOHYDRATE CHOICES	EXCHANGES
28	10	810	19	27	2	2 starch, 2 med. fat meat, 3 fat
11	4	170	13	1	0	2 med. fat meat

SMART MEAL, MCDONALD'S

Hamburger
Garden Salad
Herb Vinaigrette Salad Dressing,
Fat Free (1 pkt)
Milk, 1% (8 oz)
Vanilla Ice Cream Cone, Reduced Fat

Calories: 595
Fat: 17 grams
Carb Choices: 6
Exchanges: 2 starch,
1 1% milk,
2 other carb,
1 veg, 1½
med. fat meat,
1 fat

Hotcakes (plain)
Honey (1 pkt)
Orange Juice (6 oz)

Calories: 435
Fat: 7 grams
Carb Choices: 5½
Exchanges: 3½ starch,
1 fruit,
1 other carb,
1 fat

1 Carbohydrate Choice = 1 starch or 1 fruit or 1 milk exchange
* Grams of fiber subtracted from total carbohydrate

MENU ITEM	SERVING SIZE	CALORIES	CALORIES FROM FAT
PAPA JOHN'S			
CHEESE PIZZA			
☀ Original Crust Pizza, medium	1 slice	286	80
Thin Crust Pizza, medium	1 slice	220	98
GARDEN PIZZA			
Original Crust Pizza, medium	1 slice	298	100
Thin Crust Pizza, medium	1 slice	238	110
MEATS PIZZA			
Original Crust Pizza, medium	1 slice	410	160
Thin Crust Pizza, medium	1 slice	330	178
PEPPERONI PIZZA			
☀ Original Crust Pizza, medium	1 slice	310	110
Thin Crust Pizza, medium	1 slice	266	135
SAUSAGE PIZZA			
Original Crust Pizza, medium	1 slice	340	120
Thin Crust Pizza, medium	1 slice	270	130
WORKS PIZZA			
Original Crust Pizza, medium	1 slice	369	149
Thin Crust Pizza, medium	1 slice	319	166
SIDE ORDERS			
☀ Bread Sticks	1 piece (⅛ order)	170	27
☀ Cheese Sticks	1 piece (⅛ order)	160	50

☀ Smart Choice

TOTAL FAT (g)	SATURATED FAT (g)	SODIUM (mg)	PROTEIN (g)	CARBOHYDRATE (g)	CARBOHYDRATE CHOICES	EXCHANGES
9	3	540	14	37	2½	2½ starch, 1 med. fat meat
11	5	480	9	22	1½	1½ starch, 1 med. fat meat, 1 fat
11	4	570	14	36	2½	2½ starch, 1 med. fat meat, 1 fat
12	6	540	9	23	1½	1½ starch, 1 med. fat meat, 1 fat
18	7	1040	21	42	3	3 starch, 2 med. fat meat, 1 fat
20	9	919	15	23	1½	1½ starch, 2 med. fat meat, 2 fat
13	5	760	15	35	2	2 starch, 2 med. fat meat
15	7	580	11	22	1½	1½ starch, 1 med. fat meat, 2 fat
13	6	910	15	40	2½	2½ starch, 1½ med. fat meat, 1 fat
15	7	730	12	22	1½	1½ starch, 1 med. fat meat, 2 fat
17	6	840	18	37	2½	2½ starch, 2 med. fat meat, 1 fat
19	8	760	14	24	1½	1½ starch, 1½ med. fat meat, 2 fat
3	0	270	6	27	2	2 starch, ½ fat
6	2	290	7	21	1½	1½ starch, 1 fat

1 Carbohydrate Choice = 1 starch or 1 fruit or 1 milk exchange
* Grams of fiber subtracted from total carbohydrate

MENU ITEM	SERVING SIZE	CALORIES	CALORIES FROM FAT
SAUCES			
Garlic Sauce	2 Tbsp	150	140
Nacho Cheese Sauce	2 Tbsp	60	36
☀ Pizza Sauce	2 Tbsp	20	0

PIZZA HUT
BEEF PIZZA

Thin 'N Crispy® Pizza, medium	1 slice	229	99
Hand Tossed Pizza, medium	1 slice	260	81
Pan Pizza, medium	1 slice	286	117

CHEESE PIZZA

Thin 'N Crispy® Pizza, medium	1 slice	205	72
Hand Tossed Pizza, medium	1 slice	235	63
Pan Pizza, medium	1 slice	261	99

HAM PIZZA

☀ Thin 'N Crispy® Pizza, medium	1 slice	184	63
☀ Hand Tossed Pizza, medium	1 slice	213	45
Pan Pizza, medium	1 slice	239	81

ITALIAN SAUSAGE PIZZA

Thin 'N Crispy® Pizza, medium	1 slice	236	108
Hand Tossed Pizza, medium	1 slice	267	99
Pan Pizza, medium	1 slice	293	135

☀ Smart Choice

TOTAL FAT (g)	SATURATED FAT (g)	SODIUM (mg)	PROTEIN (g)	CARBOHYDRATE (g)	CARBOHYDRATE CHOICES	EXCHANGES
16	4	230	0	4	0	3 fat
4	4	226	2	0	0	1 fat
<1	0	120	0	2	0	free
11	5	709	13	21	1½	1½ starch, 1 med. fat meat, 1 fat
9	4	797	15	29	2	2 starch, 1 med. fat meat, 1 fat
13	5	677	14	28	2	2 starch, 1 med. fat meat, 1½ fat
8	4	534	11	21	1½	1½ starch, 1 high fat meat
7	4	621	13	29	2	2 starch, 1 high fat meat
11	5	501	12	28	2	2 starch, 1 high fat meat, ½ fat
7	3	591	10	21	1½	1½ starch, 1 med. fat meat
5	3	657	12	29	2	2 starch, 1 med. fat meat
9	3	537	11	28	2	2 starch, 1 med. fat meat, ½ fat
12	5	650	11	21	1½	1½ starch, 1 high fat meat, ½ fat
11	5	737	13	29	2	2 starch, 1 high fat meat, ½ fat
15	5	617	12	27	2	2 starch, 1 high fat meat, 1 fat

1 Carbohydrate Choice = 1 starch or 1 fruit or 1 milk exchange
* Grams of fiber subtracted from total carbohydrate

MENU ITEM		SERVING SIZE	CALORIES	CALORIES FROM FAT
MEAT LOVER'S® PIZZA				
Thin 'N Crispy® Pizza, medium		1 slice	288	117
☀ Hand Tossed Pizza, medium		1 slice	314	99
Pan Pizza		1 slice	340	162
PEPPERONI PIZZA				
Thin 'N Crispy® Pizza, medium		1 slice	215	90
Hand Tossed Pizza, medium		1 slice	238	72
Pan Pizza, medium		1 slice	265	108
PEPPERONI LOVER'S® PIZZA				
☀ Thin 'N Crispy® Pizza, medium		1 slice	289	144
☀ Hand Tossed Pizza, medium		1 slice	306	126
Pan Pizza, medium		1 slice	332	153
PORK TOPPING PIZZA				
Thin 'N Crispy Pizza, medium		1 slice	237	108
Hand Tossed Pizza, medium		1 slice	268	90
Pan Pizza, medium		1 slice	294	126
SUPER SUPREME PIZZA				
Thin 'N Crispy® Pizza, medium		1 slice	270	126
Hand Tossed Pizza, medium		1 slice	296	117
Pan Pizza, medium		1 slice	323	153
SUPREME PIZZA				
Thin 'N Crispy® Pizza, medium		1 slice	257	117
Hand Tossed Pizza, medium		1 slice	284	108
Pan Pizza, medium		1 slice	311	135

☀ Smart Choice

TOTAL FAT (g)	SATURATED FAT (g)	SODIUM (mg)	PROTEIN (g)	CARBOHYDRATE (g)	CARBOHYDRATE CHOICES	EXCHANGES
13	6	892	15	21	1½	1½ starch, 2 med. fat meat, ½ fat
11	6	958	17	29	2	2 starch, 2 med. fat meat
18	7	838	16	28	2	2 starch, 2 med. fat meat, 1 fat
10	4	627	11	21	1½	1½ starch, 1 high fat meat
8	4	689	12	29	2	2 starch, 1 high fat meat
12	4	569	11	28	2	2 starch, 1 high fat meat, ½ fat
16	7	862	15	22	1½	1½ starch, 2 med. fat meat
14	6	897	16	30	2	2 starch, 2 med. fat meat
17	7	777	15	28	2	2 starch, 2 med. fat meat, 1 fat
12	5	709	12	21	1½	1½ starch, 1 med. fat meat, 1 fat
10	5	797	14	29	2	2 starch, 1 med. fat meat, 1 fat
14	5	677	13	28	2	2 starch, 1 med. fat meat, 1½ fat
14	6	880	14	22	1½	1½ starch, 1½ med. fat meat, 1 fat
13	5	946	16	30	2	2 starch, 1½ med. fat meat, 1 fat
17	6	826	15	28	2	2 starch, 1½ med. fat meat, 1½ fat
13	5	795	14	21	1½	1½ starch, 1½ med. fat meat, 1 fat
12	5	884	16	30	2	2 starch, 1½ med. fat meat, ½ fat
15	6	764	15	28	2	2 starch, 1½ med. fat meat, 1 fat

1 Carbohydrate Choice = 1 starch or 1 fruit or 1 milk exchange
* Grams of fiber subtracted from total carbohydrate

MENU ITEM	SERVING SIZE	CALORIES	CALORIES FROM FAT
VEGGIE LOVER'S® PIZZA			
☀ Thin 'N Crispy® Pizza, medium	1 slice	186	63
☀ Hand Tossed Pizza, medium	1 slice	216	54
Pan Pizza, medium	1 slice	243	90
BIGFOOT™ PIZZA			
☀ Cheese Bigfoot™ Pizza, medium	1 slice (2.7 oz)	186	54
☀ Pepperoni Bigfoot™ Pizza, medium	1 slice (2.8 oz)	205	63
Pepperoni, Mushroom, & Italian Sausage Bigfoot™ Pizza, medium	1 slice (3 oz)	214	72
PERSONAL PAN PIZZA®			
Pepperoni Personal Pan Pizza®	1 pizza (9 oz)	637	252
Supreme Personal Pan Pizza®	1 pizza (11.5 oz)	722	306

POPEYE'S CHICKEN & BISCUITS
CHICKEN

	SERVING SIZE	CALORIES	CALORIES FROM FAT
☀ Breast, Mild	1 (3.7 oz)	270	143
☀ Breast, Spicy	1 (3.7 oz)	270	143
☀ Leg, Mild	1 (1.7 oz)	120	66
☀ Leg, Spicy	1 (1.7 oz)	120	66
☀ Mild Tender (chicken strip)	1 strip (1.2 oz)	110	63
☀ Spicy Tender (chicken strip)	1 strip (1.2 oz)	110	63
Thigh, Mild	1 (3.1 oz)	300	204
Thigh, Spicy	1 (3.1 oz)	300	204

☀ Smart Choice

TOTAL FAT (g)	SATURATED FAT (g)	SODIUM (mg)	PROTEIN (g)	CARBOHYDRATE (g)	CARBOHYDRATE CHOICES	EXCHANGES
7	3	545	9	22	1½	1½ starch, 1 med. fat meat
6	3	632	11	30	2	2 starch, 1 med. fat meat
10	3	512	10	29	2	2 starch, 1 med. fat meat, ½ fat
6	3	525	10	25	1½	1½ starch, 1 med. fat meat
7	3	589	10	25	1½	1½ starch, 1 med. fat meat
8	4	665	11	25	1½	1½ starch, 1 high fat meat
28	10	1340	27	64*	4	4½ starch, 3 med. fat meat, 1½ fat
34	12	1760	33	64*	4	4½ starch, 4 med. fat meat, 2 fat
16	NA	660	23	9	½	½ starch, 3 med. fat meat
16	NA	590	23	9	½	½ starch, 3 med. fat meat
7	NA	240	10	4	0	1½ med. fat meat
7	NA	240	10	4	0	1½ med. fat meat
7	NA	160	6	6	½	½ starch, 1 med. fat meat
7	NA	215	6	6	½	½ starch, 1 med. fat meat
23	NA	620	15	9	½	½ starch, 2 med. fat meat, 2½ fat
23	NA	450	15	9	½	½ starch, 2 med. fat meat, 2½ fat

1 Carbohydrate Choice = 1 starch or 1 fruit or 1 milk exchange
* Grams of fiber subtracted from total carbohydrate

MENU ITEM	SERVING SIZE	CALORIES	CALORIES FROM FAT
Wing, Mild	1 (1.6 oz)	160	96
Wing, Spicy	1 (1.6 oz)	160	96
SHRIMP			
Shrimp	1 order (2.8 oz)	250	148
SIDE ORDERS			
Biscuit	1 (2.3 oz)	250	134
☼ Cajun Rice	1 order (3.9 oz)	150	49
Coleslaw	1 order (4 oz)	149	101
☼ Corn on the Cob	1 order (5.2 oz)	127	26
French Fries	1 order (3 oz)	240	110
Onion Rings	1 order (3.1 oz)	310	174
☼ Potatoes & Gravy	1 order (3.8 oz	100	54
Red Beans & Rice	1 order (5.9 oz)	270	152
DESSERTS			
Apple Pie	1 slice (3.1 oz)	290	142

SMART MEAL, POPEYE'S CHICKEN & BISCUITS

Chicken Breast (Mild or Spicy)	**Calories:**	547
Cajun Rice	**Fat:**	24 grams
Corn on the Cob	**Carb Choices:**	2½
	Exchanges:	2½ starch, 4 med. fat meat, 1 fat

☼ Smart Choice

TOTAL FAT (g)	SATURATED FAT (g)	SODIUM (mg)	PROTEIN (g)	CARBOHYDRATE (g)	CARBOHYDRATE CHOICES	EXCHANGES
11	NA	290	9	7	½	½ starch, 1 med. fat meat, 1 fat
11	NA	290	9	7	½	½ starch, 1 med. fat meat, 1 fat
17	NA	650	16	13	1	1 starch, 2 med. fat meat, 1 fat
15	NA	430	4	26	2	2 starch, 3 fat
5	NA	1260	10	17	1	1 starch, 1 med. fat meat
11	NA	271	1	14	1	3 veg or 1 starch, 2 fat
3	NA	20	4	12*	1	1 starch, 1 fat
12	NA	610	4	31	2	2 starch, 2 fat
19	NA	210	5	31	2	2 starch, 3½ fat
6	NA	460	5	11	1	1 starch, 1 fat
17	NA	680	8	23*	1½	1½ starch, 1 med. fat meat, 2 fat
16	NA	820	3	37	2½	2½ other carb, 3 fat

1 Carbohydrate Choice = 1 starch or 1 fruit or 1 milk exchange
* Grams of fiber subtracted from total carbohydrate

MENU ITEM	SERVING SIZE	CALORIES	CALORIES FROM FAT
ROY ROGERS			
SANDWICHES			
Bacon Cheeseburger	1 (5.5 oz)	520	297
Cheeseburger	1 (4.9 oz)	393	198
Cheesesteak Sandwich	1 (7.6 oz)	580	324
Fish Sandwich	1 (6.5 oz)	490	189
Gold Rush Chicken Sandwich	1 (6.6 oz)	558	270
☀ Grilled Chicken Sandwich	1 (7.5 oz)	294	72
Hamburger	1 (4.4 oz)	343	162
Quarter Pound Cheeseburger	1 (5.2 oz)	480	261
Quarter Pound Hamburger	1 (4.7 oz)	412	225
☀ Roast Beef Sandwich	1 (6.7 oz)	329	90
CHICKEN			
Chicken Nuggets, 6-piece	1 order (4 oz)	290	162
☀ Fried Chicken Breast	1 (5.2 oz)	370	135
☀ Fried Chicken Leg	1 (2.4 oz)	170	63
Fried Chicken Thigh	1 (4.2 oz)	330	135
Fried Chicken Wing	1 (2.3 oz)	200	72
Roy's Roaster™ (dark meat), ¼ chicken	1 (5 oz)	490	306
☀ Roy's Roaster™ (dark meat, without skin), ¼ chicken	1 (3.9 oz)	190	90
Roy's Roaster™ (white meat), ¼ chicken	1 (6.1 oz)	500	261
☀ Roy's Roaster™ (white meat, without skin), ¼ chicken	1 (4.7 oz)	190	54

☀ Smart Choice

TOTAL FAT (g)	SATURATED FAT (g)	SODIUM (mg)	PROTEIN (g)	CARBOHYDRATE (g)	CARBOHYDRATE CHOICES	EXCHANGES
33	13	1620	24	32	2	2 starch, 3 med. fat meat, 3 fat
22	12	1405	19	32	2	2 starch, 2 med. fat meat, 2 fat
36	14	860	26	37	2½	2½ starch, 3 med. fat meat, 4 fat
21	5	1048	21	56	4	4 starch, 2 med. fat meat, 2 fat
30	9	1326	22	51	3½	3½ starch, 2½ med. fat meat, 2 fat
8	3	864	26	29	2	2 starch, 3 lean meat
18	9	1168	15	32	2	2 starch, 2 med. fat meat, 1 fat
29	17	1509	23	32	2	2 starch, 3 med. fat meat, 2½ fat
25	14	1264	20	32	2	2 starch, 2½ med. fat meat, 2 fat
10	3	975	31	29	2	2 starch, 4 lean meat
18	4	610	12	20	1	1 starch, 1½ med. fat meat, 2 fat
15	4	1190	29	29	2	2 starch, 3 med. fat meat
7	2	570	13	15	1	1 starch, 1½ med. fat meat
15	4	1000	19	30	2	2 starch, 2 med. fat meat, 1 fat
8	3	740	10	23	1½	1½ starch, 1 high fat meat
34	10	1120	43	2	0	6 med. fat meat, 1 fat
10	3	400	24	1	0	3½ lean meat
29	9	1450	56	3	0	8 lean meat, 1 fat
6	2	700	32	2	0	4½ very lean meat

1 Carbohydrate Choice = 1 starch or 1 fruit or 1 milk exchange
* Grams of fiber subtracted from total carbohydrate

MENU ITEM	SERVING SIZE	CALORIES	CALORIES FROM FAT
SIDE ORDERS			
☀ Baked Beans	1 order (5 oz)	160	18
☀ Baked Potato	1 (3.9 oz)	130	9
Baked Potato with Margarine	1 (4.3 oz)	240	117
Cole Slaw	1 order (5 oz)	295	225
French Fries, regular	1 order (5 oz)	350	135
French Fries, large	1 order (6.1 oz)	430	162
☀ Gravy	1 (1.5 oz)	20	0
☀ Mashed Potatoes	1 order (5 oz)	92	0
SOUPS			
☀ Chicken Soup	10.6 oz	225	63
☀ Chili	10.1 oz	295	135
SALADS			
☀ Garden Salad	1 (9.7 oz)	110	45
☀ Grilled Chicken Salad	1 (13.2 oz)	221	81
☀ Side Salad	1 (4.9 oz)	20	0
DESSERTS			
Hot Fudge Sundae	1 (5.9 oz)	320	80
Strawberry Shortcake	1 (6 oz)	440	171
Strawberry Sundae	1 (5.5 oz)	260	54
☀ Vanilla Frozen Yogurt Cone	1 (4.1oz)	190	36
BREAKFAST			
Bacon & Egg Biscuit	1 (4.2 oz)	470	234

☀ Smart Choice

TOTAL FAT (g)	SATURATED FAT (g)	SODIUM (mg)	PROTEIN (g)	CARBOHYDRATE (g)	CARBOHYDRATE CHOICES	EXCHANGES
2	1	560	6	30	2	2 starch
1	0	65	3	27	2	2 starch
13	2	220	3	27	2	2 starch, 2 fat
25	4	430	2	16	1	3 veg or 1 starch, 5 fat
15	4	150	5	49	3	3 starch, 3 fat
18	5	190	6	59	4	4 starch, 3 fat
<1	<1	260	<1	3	0	free
<1	<1	320	2	20	1	1 starch
7	2	1580	16	24	1½	1½ starch, 2 lean meat
15	7	1607	15	30	2	2 starch, 2 med. fat meat
5	3	348	8	10	½	2 veg or ½ starch, 1 med. fat meat
9	4	851	29	10	½	2 veg or ½ starch, 4 lean meat
<1	<1	20	1	3	0	free
10	3	260	8	50	3	3 other carb, 2 fat
19	5	620	8	39	2½	2½ other carb, 4 fat
6	3	95	6	44	3	3 other carb, 1 fat
4	3	80	6	29	2	2 other carb, 1 fat
26	8	1190	14	44	3	3 starch, 1½ med. fat meat, 3 fat

1 Carbohydrate Choice = 1 starch or 1 fruit or 1 milk exchange
* Grams of fiber subtracted from total carbohydrate

MENU ITEM	SERVING SIZE	CALORIES	CALORIES FROM FAT
Bacon Biscuit	1 (3.1 oz)	420	207
Big Breakfast Platter™ with Ham	1 (9.3 oz)	710	351
Big Country Breakfast Platter™ with Bacon	1 (7.6 oz)	740	387
Big Country Breakfast Platter™ with Sausage	1 (9.6 oz)	920	540
Biscuit	1 (2.9 oz)	390	189
Biscuits 'N' Gravy™	1 (7.7 oz)	510	252
Cinnamon 'N' Raisin™ Biscuit	1 (2.8 oz)	370	162
Ham & Cheese Biscuit	1 (4.4 oz)	450	216
Ham, Egg & Cheese Biscuit	1 (5.6 oz)	500	243
☀️ Orange Juice	10.2 oz	140	0
Sausage & Egg Biscuit	1 (5.2 oz)	560	315
Sausage Biscuit	1 (4.1 oz)	510	279
Sourdough Ham, Egg & Cheese Biscuit	1 (6.8 oz)	480	216
☀️ Pancakes (3)	1 (4.8 oz)	280	18
Pancakes (3) with Sausage (1 piece)	1 (6.2 oz)	430	144
Pancakes (3) with Bacon (2 pieces)	1 (5.3 oz)	350	81

SMART MEAL, ROY ROGERS

Roast Beef Sandwich	**Calories:**	509
Baked Beans	**Fat:**	12 grams
Side Salad	**Carb Choices:**	4
	Exchanges:	4 starch, 4 lean meat

 Smart Choice

TOTAL FAT (g)	SATURATED FAT (g)	SODIUM (mg)	PROTEIN (g)	CARBOHYDRATE (g)	CARBOHYDRATE CHOICES	EXCHANGES
23	7	1140	9	44	3	3 starch, 1 high fat meat, 2 fat
39	11	2210	24	67	4½	4½ starch, 2 med. fat meat, 5 fat
43	13	1800	35	61	4	4 starch, 4 med. fat meat, 3 fat
60	19	2230	33	61	4	4 starch, 4 med. fat meat, 7 fat
21	6	1000	6	44	3	3 starch, 4 fat
28	9	1500	10	55	3½	3½ starch, 5½ fat
18	5	450	3	48	3	3 starch, 3 fat
24	8	1570	11	48	3	3 starch, 1 med. fat meat, 3 fat
27	10	1620	16	48	3	3 starch, 2 med. fat meat, 3 fat
<1	<1	0	2	35	2	2 fruit
35	11	1400	18	44	3	3 starch, 2 med. fat meat, 4 fat
31	10	1360	14	44	3	3 starch, 1 high fat meat, 4 fat
24	9	1440	20	45	3	3 starch, 2 med. fat meat, 2 fat
2	1	890	8	56	4	4 starch
16	6	1290	16	56	4	4 starch, 1 high fat meat, 1 fat
9	3	1130	13	56	4	4 starch, 1 high fat meat

SMART MEAL, ROY ROGERS

¼ Roy Rogers Roaster™
  (white meat, without skin)
Baked Potato
Margarine (1 pat)
Side Salad
Low-calorie Dressing

Calories: 415
Fat: 14 grams
Carb Choices: 2
Exchanges: 2 starch, 4½ very lean meat, 1 fat

1 Carbohydrate Choice = 1 starch or 1 fruit or 1 milk exchange
* Grams of fiber subtracted from total carbohydrate

MENU ITEM	SERVING SIZE	CALORIES	CALORIES FROM FAT

SUBWAY
COLD SUBS

B.L.T. Sub, 6-inch	1	327	90
Classic Italian B.M.T.® Sub, 6-inch	1	460	198
☀ Cold Cut Trio Sub, 6-inch	1	378	117
☀ Ham Sub, 6-inch	1	302	45
☀ Roast Beef Sub, 6-inch	1	303	45
☀ Subway Club® Sub, 6-inch	1	312	45
Subway Seafood & Crab® Sub, 6-inch	1	430	171
☀ Subway Seafood & Crab® with Light Mayonnaise Sub, 6-inch	1	347	90
Tuna Sub, 6-inch	1	542	288
☀ Tuna with Light Mayonnaise Sub, 6-inch	1	391	135
☀ Turkey Breast Sub, 6-inch	1	289	36
☀ Turkey Breast & Ham Sub, 6-inch	1	295	45
☀ Veggie Delite™ Sub, 6-inch	1	237	27

HOT SUBS

Chicken Taco Sub, 6-inch	1	436	144
☀ Meatball Sub, 6-inch	1	419	144
Pizza Sub	1	464	198
☀ Roasted Chicken Breast Sub, 6-inch	1	348	54
☀ Steak & Cheese Sub, 6-inch	1	398	90
☀ Subway Melt™ Sub, 6-inch	1	382	108

☀ Smart Choice

TOTAL FAT (g)	SATURATED FAT (g)	SODIUM (mg)	PROTEIN (g)	CARBOHYDRATE (g)	CARBOHYDRATE CHOICES	EXCHANGES
10	NA	957	14	44	3	3 starch, 1 high fat meat
22	NA	1664	21	45	3	3 starch, 2 med. fat meat, 2 fat
13	NA	1412	20	46	3	3 starch, 2 med. fat meat
5	NA	1319	19	45	3	3 starch, 2 very lean meat
5	NA	939	20	45	3	3 starch, 2 very lean meat
5	NA	1352	21	46	3	3 starch, 2 very lean meat
19	NA	860	20	44	3	3 starch, 2 med. fat meat, 1 fat
10	NA	884	20	45	3	3 starch, 2 lean meat
32	NA	886	19	44	3	3 starch, 2 med. fat meat, 4 fat
15	NA	940	19	46	3	3 starch, 2 med. fat meat
4	NA	1403	18	46	3	3 starch, 2 very lean meat
5	NA	1361	18	46	3	3 starch, 2 very lean meat
3	NA	593	9	44	3	3 starch
16	NA	1275	25	49	3	3 starch, 2 med. fat meat, 1 fat
16	NA	1046	19	51	3½	3½ starch, 2 med. fat meat
22	NA	1621	19	48	3	3 starch, 2 med. fat meat, 2 fat
6	NA	978	27	47	3	3 starch, 3 very lean meat
10	NA	1117	30	47	3	3 starch, 3 lean meat
12	NA	1746	23	46	3	3 starch, 2 med. fat meat

1 Carbohydrate Choice = 1 starch or 1 fruit or 1 milk exchange
* Grams of fiber subtracted from total carbohydrate

MENU ITEM	SERVING SIZE	CALORIES	CALORIES FROM FAT
DELI STYLE SANDWICHES			
Bologna Sandwich, 6-inch	1	292	108
☀ Ham Sandwich, 6-inch	1	234	36
☀ Roast Beef Sandwich, 6-inch	1	245	36
Tuna Sandwich, 6-inch	1	354	162
Tuna with Light Mayonnaise Sandwich, 6-inch	1	279	81
☀ Turkey Breast Sandwich, 6-inch	1	235	36
SALADS			
B.L.T. Salad	1	140	72
☀ Bread Bowl	1	330	36
Chicken Taco Salad	1	250	126
Classic Italian B.M.T.® Salad	1	274	180
Cold Cut Trio Salad	1	191	99
☀ Ham Salad	1	116	27
Meatball Salad	1	233	126
Pizza Salad	1	277	180
☀ Roast Beef Salad	1	117	27
☀ Roasted Chicken Breast Salad	1	162	36
☀ Steak & Cheese Salad	1	212	72
☀ Subway Club Salad	1	126	27
☀ Subway Melt™ Salad	1	195	90
Subway Seafood & Crab® Salad	1	244	153

☀ Smart Choice

TOTAL FAT (g)	SATURATED FAT (g)	SODIUM (mg)	PROTEIN (g)	CARBOHYDRATE (g)	CARBOHYDRATE CHOICES	EXCHANGES
12	NA	744	10	38	2½	2½ starch, 1 med. fat meat, 1 fat
4	NA	733	11	37	2½	2½ starch, 1 lean meat
4	NA	638	13	38	2½	2½ starch, 1 lean meat
18	NA	557	11	37	2½	2½ starch, 1 med. fat meat, 2 fat
9	NA	583	11	38	2½	2½ starch, 1 lean meat, 1 fat
4	NA	944	12	38	2½	2½ starch, 1 lean meat
8	NA	672	7	10	½	2 veg, 2 fat
4	NA	760	12	63	4	4 starch
14	NA	990	18	15	1	3 veg or 1 starch, 2 med. fat meat, 1 fat
20	NA	1379	14	11	1	2 veg, 2 med. fat meat, 2 fat
11	NA	1127	13	11	1	2 veg, 1 med. fat meat, 1 fat
3	NA	1034	12	11	1	2 veg, 1 lean meat
14	NA	761	12	16	1	3 veg or 1 starch, 1 med. fat meat, 2 fat
20	NA	1336	12	13	1	3 veg or 1 starch, 1 med. fat meat, 3 fat
3	NA	654	12	11	1	2 veg, 1 lean meat
4	NA	693	20	13	1	3 veg or 1 starch, 2 lean meat
8	NA	832	22	13	1	3 veg or 1 starch, 2 med. fat meat
3	NA	1067	14	12	1	2 veg, 2 very lean meat
10	NA	1461	16	12	1	2 veg, 2 med. fat meat
17	NA	575	13	10	½	2 veg, 2 med. fat meat, 1 fat

1 Carbohydrate Choice = 1 starch or 1 fruit or 1 milk exchange
* Grams of fiber subtracted from total carbohydrate

MENU ITEM	SERVING SIZE	CALORIES	CALORIES FROM FAT
Subway Seafood & Crab with Light Mayonnaise Salad	1	161	72
Tuna Salad	1	356	270
Tuna with Light Mayonnaise Salad	1	205	117
🔆 Turkey Breast Salad	1	102	18
🔆 Turkey Breast & Ham Salad	1	109	27
🔆 Veggie Delite™ Salad	1	51	9
SALAD DRESSINGS			
🔆 Creamy Italian Salad Dressing	1 Tbsp	65	54
🔆 French Salad Dressing	1 Tbsp	65	45
🔆 French Salad Dressing, Fat Free	1 Tbsp	15	0
🔆 Italian Salad Dressing, Fat Free	1 Tbsp	5	0
Ranch Salad Dressing	1 Tbsp	87	81
🔆 Ranch Salad Dressing, Fat Free	1 Tbsp	12	0
🔆 Thousand Island Salad Dressing	1 Tbsp	65	54
CONDIMENTS			
Bacon	2 pieces	45	36
Cheese	2 triangles	41	27
Mayonnaise	1 tsp	37	36
🔆 Mayonnaise, Light	1 tsp	18	18
🔆 Mustard	2 tsp	8	0
Olive Oil Blend	1 tsp	45	45
🔆 Vinegar	1 tsp	1	0

🔆 Smart Choice

TOTAL FAT (g)	SATURATED FAT (g)	SODIUM (mg)	PROTEIN (g)	CARBOHYDRATE (g)	CARBOHYDRATE CHOICES	EXCHANGES
8	NA	599	13	11	1	2 veg, 1 med. fat meat, 1 fat
30	NA	601	12	10	½	2 veg, 1 med. fat meat, 5 fat
13	NA	654	12	11	1	2 veg, 1 med. fat meat, 2 fat
2	NA	1117	11	12	1	2 veg, 1 lean meat
3	NA	1076	11	11	1	2 veg, 1 lean meat
1	NA	308	2	10	½	½ starch or 2 veg
6	NA	132	0	2	0	1 fat
5	NA	100	0	5	0	1 fat
0	NA	85	0	4	0	free
0	NA	152	0	1	0	free
9	NA	117	0	1	0	2 fat
0	NA	177	0	3	0	free
6	NA	107	0	2	0	1 fat
4	NA	182	2	0	0	1 fat
3	NA	204	2	0	0	1 fat
4	NA	27	0	0	0	1 fat
2	NA	33	0	0	0	free
0	NA	0	1	1	0	free
5	NA	0	0	0	0	1 fat
0	NA	0	0	0	0	free

1 Carbohydrate Choice = 1 starch or 1 fruit or 1 milk exchange
* Grams of fiber subtracted from total carbohydrate

MENU ITEM	SERVING SIZE	CALORIES	CALORIES FROM FAT
COOKIES			
Chocolate Chip Cookie	1	210	90
Chocolate Chip M&M® Cookie	1	210	90
Chocolate Chunk Cookie	1	210	90
Double Chocolate Brazil Nut Cookie	1	230	108
☀ Oatmeal Raisin Cookie	1	200	72
Peanut Butter Cookie	1	220	108
Sugar Cookie	1	230	108
White Chocolate Macadamia Nut Cookie	1	230	108

SMART MEAL, SUBWAY

Subway Club® Sub, 6-inch
Veggie Delite™ Salad
Ranch Salad Dressing, Fat Free

Calories:	375
Fat:	6 grams
Carb Choices:	4
Exchanges:	3 starch, 2 veg, 2 very lean meat

☀ Smart Choice

TOTAL FAT (g)	SATURATED FAT (g)	SODIUM (mg)	PROTEIN (g)	CARBOHYDRATE (g)	CARBOHYDRATE CHOICES	EXCHANGES
10	NA	140	2	29	2	2 other carb, 1½ fat
10	NA	140	2	29	2	2 other carb, 1½ fat
10	NA	140	2	29	2	2 other carb, 1½ fat
12	NA	115	3	27	2	2 other carb, 2 fat
8	NA	160	3	29	2	2 other carb, 1 fat
12	NA	180	3	26	2	2 other carb, 2 fat
12	NA	180	2	28	2	2 other carb, 2 fat
12	NA	140	2	28	2	2 other carb, 2 fat

SMART MEAL, SUBWAY

Roast Beef Salad in a Bread Bowl
Italian Salad Dressing, Fat Free (4 Tbsp)

Calories: 467
Fat: 7 grams
Carb Choices: 5
Exchanges: 4 starch,
2 veg,
1 lean meat

1 Carbohydrate Choice = 1 starch *or* 1 fruit *or* 1 milk exchange
* Grams of fiber subtracted from total carbohydrate

MENU ITEM	SERVING SIZE	CALORIES	CALORIES FROM FAT

TACO BELL
TACOS

BLT Soft Taco	1 (4.25 oz)	340	210
Double Decker™ Taco	1 (5.5 oz)	340	130
Double Decker™ Taco Supreme®	1 (6.75 oz)	390	170
Kid's Soft Taco Roll-Up	1 (3.75 oz)	290	140
Soft Taco	1 (3.5 oz)	210	90
Soft Taco Supreme®	1 (4.75 oz)	260	120
☼ Steak Soft Taco	1 (5 oz)	200	60
Taco	1 (2.75 oz)	170	90
Taco Supreme®	1 (4 oz)	220	120

BURRITOS

Bacon Cheeseburger Burrito	1 (8.25)	560	270
Bean Burrito	1 (7 oz)	380	110
Big Beef Burrito Supreme®	1 (10.25 oz)	520	210
Burrito Supreme®	1 (8.75 oz)	440	170
Chicken Club Burrito	1 (7.75 oz)	540	280
Chili Cheese Burrito	1 (5 oz)	330	120
Seven-Layer Burrito	1 (10 oz)	540	210

SPECIALTIES

Big Beef MexiMelt®	1 (4.5 oz)	300	150
Cheese Quesadilla	1 (4.25 oz)	370	180
Chicken Quesadilla	1 (5.75 oz)	420	190
Mexican Pizza	1 (7.75 oz)	570	330

☼ Smart Choice

TOTAL FAT (g)	SATURATED FAT (g)	SODIUM (mg)	PROTEIN (g)	CARBOHYDRATE (g)	CARBOHYDRATE CHOICES	EXCHANGES
23	8	610	11	22	1½	1½ starch, 1 med. fat meat, 3½ fat
15	5	700	16	29*	2	2 starch, 2 med. fat meat, 2 fat
18	8	710	16	31*	2	2 starch, 2 med. fat meat, 1 fat
16	8	790	16	20	1	1 starch, 2 med. fat meat, 1 fat
10	5	530	12	20	1	1 starch, 1 med. fat meat, 1 fat
14	7	540	13	22	1½	1½ starch, 1 med. fat meat, 2 fat
7	3	500	14	18	1	1 starch, 2 lean meat
10	4	280	10	11	1	1 starch, 1 med. fat meat, 1 fat
13	6	290	11	13	1	1 starch, 1 med. fat meat, 1½ fat
30	12	1360	29	43	3	3 starch, 3 med. fat meat, 2½ fat
12	4	1140	13	43*	3	3 starch, 1 med. fat meat, 1 fat
23	10	1450	26	43*	3	3 starch, 3 med. fat meat, 1½ fat
18	8	1220	19	42*	3	3 starch, 2 med. fat meat, 1½ fat
31	10	1290	22	43	3	3 starch, 2 med. fat meat, 4 fat
13	6	880	14	37	2½	2½ starch, 1 med. fat meat, 1½ fat
24	9	1310	16	51*	3½	3½ starch, 1½ med. fat meat, 3 fat
16	8	860	16	21	1½	1½ starch, 2 med. fat meat, 1 fat
20	12	730	16	32	2	2 starch, 1½ med. fat meat, 2 fat
22	12	1020	24	33	2	2 starch, 3 med. fat meat, 1 fat
36	11	1050	21	35*	2	2 starch, 2½ med. fat meat, 5 fat

1 Carbohydrate Choice = 1 starch or 1 fruit or 1 milk exchange
* Grams of fiber subtracted from total carbohydrate

MENU ITEM	SERVING SIZE	CALORIES	CALORIES FROM FAT
Taco Salad with Salsa	1 (19 oz)	840	470
Taco Salad with Salsa (without shell)	1 (16 oz)	420	190
Tostada	1 (6.25 oz)	300	130
BORDER WRAPS™			
Chicken Fajita Wrap™	1 (7.75 oz)	460	190
Chicken Fajita Wrap™ Supreme	1 (9 oz)	500	230
Steak Fajita Wrap™	1 (7.75 oz)	460	190
Steak Fajita Wrap™ Supreme	1 (9 oz)	510	230
Veggie Fajita Wrap™	1 (7.75 oz)	420	170
Veggie Fajita Wrap™ Supreme	1 (9 oz)	460	210
BORDER LIGHTS™			
☀ Light Chicken Burrito	1 (6.25 oz)	310	70
Light Chicken Burrito Supreme®	1 (8.75 oz)	430	120
☀ Light Chicken Soft Taco	1 (4.25 oz)	180	45
☀ Light Kid's Chicken Soft Taco	1 (3.5 oz)	180	45
SIDE ORDERS			
Big Beef Nachos Supreme	1 order (6.75 oz)	430	210
☀ Cinnamon Twists	1 order (1 oz)	140	50
Mexican Rice	1 order (4.75 oz)	190	90
Nachos	1 order (3.5 oz)	310	160
Nachos BellGrande®	1 order (10.75 oz)	740	350
☀ Pintos 'n Cheese	1 order (4.5 oz)	190	80

☀ Smart Choice

TOTAL FAT (g)	SATURATED FAT (g)	SODIUM (mg)	PROTEIN (g)	CARBOHYDRATE (g)	CARBOHYDRATE CHOICES	EXCHANGES
52	15	1670	32	49*	3½	3½ starch, 3 med. fat meat, 7 fat
21	11	1420	26	16*	1	1 starch, 2 med. fat meat, 1 fat
14	5	700	11	20*	1½	1½ starch, 1 med. fat meat, 2 fat
21	6	1220	18	49	3	3 starch, 2 med. fat meat, 2 fat
25	8	1230	19	51	3½	3½ starch, 2 med. fat meat, 2 fat
21	6	1130	20	48	3	3 starch, 2 med. fat meat, 2 fat
25	8	1140	21	50	3	3 starch, 2 med. fat meat, 3 fat
19	5	920	11	51	3½	3 starch, 1 veg, 3 fat
23	8	930	11	53	3½	3 starch, 1 veg, 2½ fat
8	2	980	18	41	3	3 starch, 2 lean meat
13	3	1410	25	52	3½	3½ starch, 2 lean meat, 1 fat
5	2	660	13	21	1½	1½ starch, 1½ lean meat
5	2	590	13	20	1½	1½ starch, 1½ lean meat
24	7	720	12	34*	2	2 starch, 1 med. fat meat, 4 fat
6	0	190	1	19	1	1 starch, 1 fat
10	4	510	6	20	1	1 starch, 2 fat
18	4	540	2	34	2	2 starch, 3½ fat
39	10	1200	16	66*	4½	4½ starch, 1 med. fat meat, 7 fat
8	4	690	9	8*	½	½ starch, 1 med. fat meat, 1 fat

1 Carbohydrate Choice = 1 starch or 1 fruit or 1 milk exchange
* Grams of fiber subtracted from total carbohydrate

MENU ITEM	SERVING SIZE	CALORIES	CALORIES FROM FAT
CONDIMENTS			
☼ Cheddar Cheese	.25 oz	30	20
☼ Cheddar Cheese, Fat Free	.25 oz	10	0
☼ Green Sauce	1 oz	5	0
Guacamole	1.5 oz	70	50
☼ Hot Taco Sauce	.33 oz	0	0
☼ Mild Taco Sauce	.33 oz	0	0
Nacho Cheese Sauce	2 oz	120	90
☼ Pepper Jack Cheese	.25 oz	30	25
☼ Picante Sauce	.33 oz	0	0
☼ Pico de Gallo	.75 oz	5	0
☼ Red Sauce	1 oz	10	0
☼ Salsa	3 oz	25	0
Sour Cream	.75 oz	40	35
☼ Sour Cream, Non-Fat	.75 oz	20	0
SOFT DRINKS			
Diet Pepsi®	16 oz	0	0
Dr. Pepper®	16 oz	208	0
Mountain Dew®	16 oz	227	0
Pepsi Cola®	16 oz	200	0
Slice®	16 oz	200	0
OTHER BEVERAGES			
C̶o̶f̶f̶e̶e̶	12 oz	5	0
Iced Tea (sweetened)	16 oz	140	0

TOTAL FAT (g)	SATURATED FAT (g)	SODIUM (mg)	PROTEIN (g)	CARBOHYDRATE (g)	CARBOHYDRATE CHOICES	EXCHANGES
2	2	45	2	0	0	free
0	0	50	2	0	0	free
0	0	150	0	1	0	free
6	<1	280	0	4	0	1 fat
0	0	85	0	0	0	free
0	0	75	0	0	0	free
10	3	470	2	5	0	2 fat
2	1	105	1	0	0	free
0	0	110	0	1	0	free
0	0	65	0	1	0	free
0	0	260	0	2	0	free
0	0	490	1	5	0	free
4	3	10	1	1	0	1 fat
0	0	55	1	2	0	free
0	0	47	0	0	0	free
0	0	9	0	52	3½	3½ other carb
0	0	93	0	61	4	4 other carb
0	0	47	0	51	3½	3½ other carb
0	0	73	0	53	3½	3½ other carb
0	0	5	0	1	0	free
0	0	60	0	40	2½	2½ other carb

1 Carbohydrate Choice = 1 starch or 1 fruit or 1 milk exchange
* Grams of fiber subtracted from total carbohydrate

MENU ITEM

	SERVING SIZE	CALORIES	CALORIES FROM FAT
Lipton® Brisk Iced Tea (unsweetened)	16 oz	0	0
☀ Milk, 2%	8 oz	110	40
☀ Orange Juice	6 oz	80	0
BREAKFAST			
Breakfast Cheese Quesadilla	1 (5.5 oz)	390	200
Breakfast Quesadilla with Bacon	1 (6 oz)	460	250
Breakfast Quesadilla with Sausage	1 (6 oz)	440	240
Country Breakfast Burrito	1 (4 oz)	270	130
Double Bacon & Egg Burrito	1 (6.25 oz)	480	250
Fiesta Breakfast Burrito	1 (3.5 oz)	280	140
Grande Breakfast Burrito	1 (6.25 oz)	420	200

SMART MEAL, TACO BELL

Light Chicken Burrito	**Calories:**	605
Salsa (3 oz)	**Fat:**	16 grams
Pintos 'n Cheese	**Carb Choices:**	5
Orange Juice (6 oz)	**Exchanges:**	3½ starch, 1 fruit, 3 med. fat meat

☀ Smart Choice

TOTAL FAT (g)	SATURATED FAT (g)	SODIUM (mg)	PROTEIN (g)	CARBOHYDRATE (g)	CARBOHYDRATE CHOICES	EXCHANGES
0	0	60	0	0	0	free
5	3	115	8	11	1	1 2% milk
0	0	0	1	18	1	1 fruit
22	10	940	15	32	2	2 starch, 2 med. fat meat, 2 fat
28	12	1130	20	33	2	2 starch, 2½ med. fat meat, 3 fat
26	12	1010	17	33	2	2 starch, 2 med. fat meat, 3 fat
14	5	690	8	26	2	2 starch, 1 med. fat meat, 1 fat
27	9	1240	18	39	2½	2½ starch, 2 med. fat meat, 3 fat
16	6	590	9	25	1½	1½ starch, 1 med. fat meat, 2 fat
22	7	1050	13	43	3	3 starch, 1 med. fat meat, 3 fat

1 Carbohydrate Choice = 1 starch or 1 fruit or 1 milk exchange
* Grams of fiber subtracted from total carbohydrate

MENU ITEM	SERVING SIZE	CALORIES	CALORIES FROM FAT

WENDY'S
SANDWICHES

Big Bacon Classic Sandwich	1 (10 oz)	570	260
☀ Breaded Chicken Sandwich	1 (7.3 oz)	440	160
Cheeseburger, Kid's Meal	1 (4.3 oz)	320	120
Chicken Club Sandwich	1 (7.6 oz)	470	180
☀ Grilled Chicken Sandwich	1 (6.6 oz)	310	70
☀ Hamburger, Kid's Meal	1 (4 oz)	270	90
Jr. Bacon Cheeseburger	1 (6 oz)	380	170
Jr. Cheeseburger	1 (4.5 oz)	320	120
Jr. Cheeseburger Deluxe	1 (6.3 oz)	360	150
☀ Jr. Hamburger	1 (4 oz)	270	90
☀ Single Hamburger, plain	1 (4.7 oz)	360	140
Single Hamburger, with everything	1 (7.7 oz)	420	180
☀ Spicy Chicken Sandwich	1 (7.5 oz)	410	130

SANDWICH INGREDIENTS

American Cheese	1 slice (0.6 oz)	70	50
American Cheese, Jr.	1 slice (0.4 oz)	45	30
Bacon	1 piece (14 oz)	20	10
Breaded Chicken Fillet	1 (3.5 oz)	230	100
☀ Grilled Chicken Fillet	1 (3 oz)	110	25
☀ Hamburger Patty	1 (¼ lb)	200	120
☀ Hamburger Patty	1 (2 oz)	100	`60

☀ Smart Choice

TOTAL FAT (g)	SATURATED FAT (g)	SODIUM (mg)	PROTEIN (g)	CARBOHYDRATE (g)	CARBOHYDRATE CHOICES	EXCHANGES
29	12	1320	34	46	3	3 starch, 4 med. fat meat, 1 fat
18	3	840	28	44	3	3 starch, 3 med. fat meat
13	6	770	17	33	2	2 starch, 1½ med. fat meat, 1 fat
20	4	980	31	44	3	3 starch, 3 med. fat meat, 1 fat
8	2	780	27	35	2	2 starch, 3 lean meat
10	3	560	15	33	2	2 starch, 1½ med. fat meat
19	7	790	21	34	2	2 starch, 2½ med. fat meat, 1 fat
13	6	770	17	34	2	2 starch, 2 med. fat meat, ½ fat
16	6	840	18	36	2½	2½ starch, 2 med. fat meat, 1 fat
10	3	560	15	34	2	2 starch, 1 med. fat meat
16	6	460	25	31	2	2 starch, 3 med. fat meat
20	7	810	26	37	2	2 starch, 1 veg, 3 med. fat meat, 1 fat
15	3	1280	28	43	3	3 starch, 3 med. fat meat
5	3	320	3	1	0	½ med. fat meat, 1 fat
4	3	220	2	0	0	1 fat
1	0	65	1	0	0	free
12	2	490	22	10	½	½ starch, 3 med. fat meat
3	1	450	22	0	0	3 very lean meat
13	6	170	20	0	0	3 med. fat meat
7	3	85	10	0	0	1 med. fat meat

1 Carbohydrate Choice = 1 starch or 1 fruit or 1 milk exchange
* Grams of fiber subtracted from total carbohydrate

MENU ITEM	SERVING SIZE	CALORIES	CALORIES FROM FAT
☀ Honey Mustard, Reduced Calorie	1 tsp	25	15
☀ Kaiser Bun	1 (2.4 oz)	190	30
☀ Ketchup	1 tsp	10	0
☀ Lettuce	1 leaf	0	0
Mayonnaise	1½ tsp	30	30
☀ Mustard	½ tsp	0	0
☀ Onion	4 rings (0.5 oz)	0	0
☀ Pickles	4 slices (0.4 oz)	0	0
☀ Sandwich Bun	1 (2 oz)	160	25
☀ Spicy Chicken Fillet	1 (3.7 oz)	210	80
☀ Tomatoes	1 slice (1 oz)	5	0

STUFFED PITAS™

Chicken Caesar Pita	1 (8.5 oz)	490	160
Classic Greek Pita	1 (8.25 oz)	430	170
☀ Garden Ranch Chicken Pita	1 (10 oz)	480	160
Garden Veggie Pita	1 (9 oz)	390	140

CHICKEN NUGGETS

Chicken Nuggets, 5-piece	1 order (2.6 oz)	210	130

BAKED POTATOES

Bacon & Cheese Potato	1 (13.4 oz)	540	160
Broccoli & Cheese Potato	1 (14.5 oz)	470	120
Cheese Potato	1 (13.4 oz)	570	210
Chili & Cheese Potato	1 (15.5 oz)	620	220

☀ Smart Choice

TOTAL FAT (g)	SATURATED FAT (g)	SODIUM (mg)	PROTEIN (g)	CARBOHYDRATE (g)	CARBOHYDRATE CHOICES	EXCHANGES
2	0	35	0	2	0	free
3	<1	340	6	36	2½	2½ starch
0	0	80	0	2	0	free
0	0	0	0	0	0	free
3	0	60	0	1	0	½ fat
0	0	55	0	0	0	free
0	0	0	0	1	0	free
0	0	140	0	0	0	free
3	<1	280	5	29	2	2 starch
9	2	920	22	10	½	½ starch, 3 med. fat meat
0	0	0	0	1	0	free
17	5	1300	36	46	3	3 starch, 4 lean meat, 1 fat
19	7	1070	17	49	3	3 starch, 2 med. fat meat, 1 fat
17	4	1170	32	44*	3	3 starch, 4 lean meat
15	3	780	13	45*	3	3 starch, 1 med. fat meat, 2 fat
14	3	460	14	7	½	½ other carb, 2 med. fat meat, 1 fat
18	4	1430	17	71*	5	5 starch, 3 fat
14	3	470	9	71*	5	5 starch, 2 fat
23	9	640	14	71*	5	5 starch, 5 fat
24	9	780	20	74*	5	5 starch, 1½ med. fat meat, 3 fat

1 Carbohydrate Choice = 1 starch or 1 fruit or 1 milk exchange
* Grams of fiber subtracted from total carbohydrate

MENU ITEM	SERVING SIZE	CALORIES	CALORIES FROM FAT
☀ Plain Potato	1 (10 oz)	310	0
☀ Sour Cream & Chives Potato	1 (11 oz)	380	60
SIDE ORDERS			
French Fries, small	1 order (3.2 oz)	260	120
French Fries, medium	1 order (4.6 oz)	380	170
French Fries, Biggie	1 order (5.6 oz)	460	200
CHILI			
☀ Chili, small	8 oz	210	60
☀ Chile, large	12 oz	310	90
SALADS			
☀ Caesar Side Salad	1 (3 oz)	110	40
Deluxe Garden Salad	1 (10 oz)	110	50
☀ Grilled Chicken Caesar Salad	1 (9 oz)	260	90
☀ Grilled Chicken Salad	1 (12 oz)	200	70
☀ Side Salad	1 (5.5 oz)	60	25
Taco Salad	1 (7.4 oz)	590	270
SALAD DRESSINGS			
Blue Cheese Salad Dressing	2 Tbsp	170	170
French Salad Dressing	2 Tbsp	120	90
☀ French Salad Dressing, Fat Free	2 Tbsp	30	0
French Salad Dressing, Sweet Red	2 Tbsp	130	90
Hidden Valley® Ranch Salad Dressing	2 Tbsp	90	90
☀ Hidden Valley® Ranch Salad Dressing, Reduced Fat, Reduced Calorie	2 Tbsp	60	50

☀ Smart Choice

TOTAL FAT (g)	SATURATED FAT (g)	SODIUM (mg)	PROTEIN (g)	CARBOHYDRATE (g)	CARBOHYDRATE CHOICES	EXCHANGES
0	0	25	7	64*	4	4 starch
6	4	40	8	66*	4½	4½ starch, 1 fat
13	3	85	3	33	2	2 starch, 2 fat
19	4	120	5	42*	3	3 starch, 3 fat
23	5	150	6	52*	4	4 starch, 4 fat
7	3	800	15	16*	1	1 starch, 2 med. fat meat
10	4	1190	23	25*	2	2 starch, 3 med. fat meat
5	2	660	8	8	½	1 veg, 1 med. fat meat
6	1	320	7	10	½	2 veg, 1 fat
10	3	1210	28	17	1	3 veg, 3 lean meat
8	2	690	25	10	½	2 veg, 3 lean meat
3	<1	160	4	5	0	1 veg
30	11	1230	29	43*	3	3 starch, 3 med. fat meat, 3 fat
19	3	190	1	0	0	4 fat
10	2	330	0	6	0	2 fat
0	0	150	0	8	½	½ starch
10	2	230	0	9	½	½ starch, 2 fat
10	2	240	0	1	0	2 fat
5	1	240	0	2	0	1 fat

1 Carbohydrate Choice = 1 starch or 1 fruit or 1 milk exchange
* Grams of fiber subtracted from total carbohydrate

MENU ITEM	SERVING SIZE	CALORIES	CALORIES FROM FAT
Italian Caesar	2 Tbsp	150	140
☀ Italian Salad Dressing, Reduced Fat, Reduced Calorie	2 Tbsp	40	30
Salad Oil	1 Tbsp	130	130
Thousand Island Salad Dressing	2 Tbsp	130	110
☀ Wine Vinegar Salad Dressing	1 Tbsp	0	0
GARDEN SPOT SALAD BAR			
☀ Applesauce	2 Tbsp	30	0
Bacon Bits	2 Tbsp	45	20
☀ Bananas & Strawberry Glaze	¼ cup	30	0
☀ Broccoli	¼ cup	0	0
☀ Cantaloupe	1 slice	15	0
☀ Carrots	¼ cup	5	0
☀ Cauliflower	¼ cup	0	0
Cheese, shredded (imitation)	2 Tbsp	50	40
Chicken Salad	2 Tbsp	70	45
☀ Chow Mein Noodles	¼ cup	35	20
Cole Slaw	2 Tbsp	45	25
☀ Cottage Cheese	2 Tbsp	30	15
☀ Croutons	2 Tbsp	30	10
☀ Cucumbers	2 slices	0	0
Eggs, hard cooked	2 Tbsp	40	25
☀ Green Peas	2 Tbsp	15	0
☀ Green Peppers	2 pieces	0	0
☀ Honeydew Melon	1 slice	20	0

☀ Smart Choice

TOTAL FAT (g)	SATURATED FAT (g)	SODIUM (mg)	PROTEIN (g)	CARBOHYDRATE (g)	CARBOHYDRATE CHOICES	EXCHANGES
16	3	250	1	1	0	3 fat
3	0	340	0	2	0	½ fat
14	2	0	0	0	0	3 fat
13	2	170	0	3	0	3 fat
0	0	0	0	0	0	free
0	0	0	0	7	½	½ fruit
3	1	570	6	0	0	1 med. fat meat
0	0	0	0	8	½	½ fruit
0	0	0	0	1	0	free
0	0	0	0	4	0	free
0	0	5	0	2	0	free
0	0	0	0	1	0	free
4	1	230	3	1	0	1 fat
5	1	135	4	2	0	1 med. fat meat
2	0	30	0	4	0	free
3	0	65	0	5	0	1 veg, 1 fat
2	1	125	4	1	0	½ lean meat
1	0	75	0	4	0	free
0	0	0	0	0	0	free
3	1	30	3	0	0	½ med. fat meat
0	0	25	1	3	0	free
0	0	0	0	1	0	free
0	0	5	0	5	0	free

1 Carbohydrate Choice = 1 starch or 1 fruit or 1 milk exchange
* Grams of fiber subtracted from total carbohydrate

MENU ITEM	SERVING SIZE	CALORIES	CALORIES FROM FAT
🔆 Lettuce (Iceberg/Romaine)	1 cup	10	0
🔆 Lettuce (Iceberg/Romaine)	3 cups	30	0
🔆 Mushrooms	¼ cup	0	0
🔆 Orange	2 slices	15	0
Parmesan Blend	2 Tbsp	70	35
🔆 Pasta Salad	2 Tbsp	25	0
🔆 Peaches	1 slice	15	0
Pepperoni	6 slices	30	25
🔆 Pineapple	4 chunks	20	0
Potato Salad	2 Tbsp	80	60
Pudding, Chocolate	¼ cup	70	30
Pudding, Vanilla	¼ cup	70	30
🔆 Red Onions	3 rings	0	0
Seafood Salad	¼ cup	70	40
🔆 Sesame Breadstick	1 (0.1 oz)	15	0
🔆 Strawberries	1 (1 oz)	10	0
Sunflower Seeds & Raisins	2 Tbsp	80	45
🔆 Tomato	1 wedge (1 oz)	5	0
Turkey Ham, diced	2 Tbsp	50	35
🔆 Watermelon	1 wedge (2 oz)	20	0
CONDIMENTS			
🔆 Barbecue Sauce	1 pkt (1 oz)	50	0
Cheddar Cheese, shredded	2 Tbsp	70	50
Honey Mustard Sauce	1 pkt (1 oz)	130	110

🔆 Smart Choice

TOTAL FAT (g)	SATURATED FAT (g)	SODIUM (mg)	PROTEIN (g)	CARBOHYDRATE (g)	CARBOHYDRATE CHOICES	EXCHANGES
0	0	5	0	2	0	free
0	0	15	0	4	0	1 veg
0	0	0	0	1	0	free
0	0	0	0	4	0	free
4	2	290	4	5	0	1 med. fat meat
0	0	75	1	3	0	free
0	0	0	0	4	0	free
3	1	70	1	0	0	½ fat
0	0	0	0	5	0	free
7	3	180	0	5	0	1 veg, 1 fat
3	<1	60	0	10	½	½ other carb, ½ fat
3	<1	60	0	10	½	½ other carb, ½ fat
0	0	0	0	1	0	free
4	<1	300	3	5	0	½ med. fat meat
0	0	20	0	2	0	free
0	0	0	0	2	0	free
5	<1	0	0	5	0	1 fat
0	0	0	0	1	0	free
4	1	280	3	0	0	1 fat
0	0	0	0	4	0	free
0	0	100	1	11	½	½ other carb
6	3	110	4	1	0	1 med. fat meat
12	2	220	0	6	½	½ other carb, 2 fat

1 Carbohydrate Choice = 1 starch or 1 fruit or 1 milk exchange
* Grams of fiber subtracted from total carbohydrate

MENU ITEM	SERVING SIZE	CALORIES	CALORIES FROM FAT
Margarine, whipped	1 pkt (0.5 oz)	60	60
☀ Saltine Crackers	2 (0.2 oz)	25	5
☀ Soft Breadstick	1 (1.5 oz)	130	30
Sour Cream	1 pkt (1 oz)	60	50
☀ Spicy Buffalo Wing Sauce	1 pkt (1 oz)	25	10
☀ Sweet & Sour Sauce	1 pkt (1 oz)	50	0
DESSERTS			
Chocolate Chip Cookie	1 (2 oz)	270	100
Frosty™ Dairy Dessert, small	1 (12 oz)	340	90
Frosty™ Dairy Dessert, medium	1 (16 oz)	460	120
Frosty™ Dairy Dessert, large	1 (20 oz)	570	150
BEVERAGES			
Coffee, black	6 oz	0	0
Hot Chocolate	6 oz	80	25
Lemonade, small	8 oz	90	0
☀ Milk, 2%	8 oz	110	40

SMART MEAL, WENDY'S

Single Hamburger with lettuce, tomato, and onions	**Calories:**	545
	Fat:	19 grams
Side Salad	**Carb Choices:**	4½ carb
French Salad Dressing, Fat Free (2 Tbsp)	**Exchanges:**	2½ starch,
Lemonade, small		1½ other carb,
		3 med. fat meat

☀ Smart Choice

TOTAL FAT (g)	SATURATED FAT (g)	SODIUM (mg)	PROTEIN (g)	CARBOHYDRATE (g)	CARBOHYDRATE CHOICES	EXCHANGES
7	1	110	0	0	0	1 fat
1	0	80	0	4	0	free
3	<1	250	4	24	1½	1½ starch
6	4	15	1	1	0	1 fat
1	0	210	0	4	0	free
0	0	120	0	12	0	1 other carb
11	8	150	4	38	2½	2½ other carb, 2 fat
10	5	200	9	57	4	4 other carb, 2 fat
13	7	260	12	76	5	5 other carb, 3 fat
17	9	330	15	90*	6	6 other carb, 4 fat
0	0	0	0	1	0	free
3	0	135	1	15	1	1 other carb
0	0	5	0	24	1½	1½ other carb
4	3	115	8	11	1	1 2% milk

SMART MEAL, WENDY'S

Chili, large
Caesar Side Salad
Wine Vinegar Salad Dressing
Soft Breadstick
Diet Soft Drink

Calories: 550
Fat: 18 grams
Carb Choices: 4
Exchanges: 3½ starch, 1 veg, 4 med. fat meat

1 Carbohydrate Choice = 1 starch or 1 fruit or 1 milk exchange
* Grams of fiber subtracted from total carbohydrate

Books of Related Interest from
IDC Publishing

Convenience Food Facts
A Quick Guide for Choosing Healthy Brand-Name Foods in Every Aisle of the Supermarket
Fourth Edition

Arlene Monk, RD, LD, CDE, and Nancy Cooper, RD, LD, CDE

Completely revised and expanded, *Convenience Food Facts* has everything you need to plan quick, healthy meals using prepared foods. This edition highlights low-fat choices among more than 4,500 popular brand-name products. Also includes carbohydrate choices and exchange values. Ideal for anyone using a meal-planning method to lose weight or to manage a health problem such as diabetes.

$12.95; ISBN 1-885115-36-9

Exchanges for All Occasions
Your Guide to Choosing Healthy Foods Anytime Anywhere
Fourth Edition

Marion J. Franz, MS, RD, LD, CDE

Exchanges for All Occasions is still the best resource there is for applying good nutrition to everyday life. Updated to reflect the new exchange lists and carbohydrate counting, this best-selling book is essential for anyone following a meal plan for weight control, diabetes, or another health condition. Includes nutrition information on over 2,500 foods, including ethnic foods, fast foods, and more.

$13.95; ISBN 1-885115-35-0

These books are available at your local bookstore.
Visit our website at www.idcpublishing.com